CONTENTS!

KV-702-453

PREFACE 1

CHAPTER 1   TEXTS   2

CHAPTER 2   NARRATIVE FICTION:
THE SHORT STORY   26

CHAPTER 3   PUNCTUATION MATTERS   78

CHAPTER 4   NARRATIVE FICTION: NOVELS   89

CHAPTER 5   NOUNS AND PRONOUNS   111

CHAPTER 6   LETTER WRITING   126

CHAPTER 7   VERBS   144

CHAPTER 8   FACTUAL TEXTS   151

CHAPTER 9   ADJECTIVES AND ADVERBS   175

CHAPTER 10   POETRY   188

CHAPTER 11   DRAMA   245

CHAPTER 12   NEWSPAPERS AND CARTOONS   269

CHAPTER 13   ADVERTISING   295

INDEX   316

ACKNOWLEDGMENTS

The author wishes to thank all the staff at Gill & Macmillan who helped make this publication possible, especially the managing editor Aoileann O'Donnell, commissioning editor Anthony Murray, and the photo editor Helen Thompson. Special thanks are also due to Noel Cahill for his contributions, advice and support during the preparation of this script.

Marie Dunne

PREFACE

New English Experience 1 offers a variety of learning experiences that show the importance of texts – how they form ideas, arouse our emotions and broaden our views of the world. Introductory chapters explain the nature and structure of texts and clearly distinguish between literary and factual text types.

Throughout the book, a wide range of literary texts is explored, including short stories, poems, plays and excerpts from novels. The personal and everyday factual texts that are presented include newspaper articles, explanations, letters, recipes, reports, interviews and advertisements.

Models of both literary and factual text types have been selected to demonstrate the important features of their structure and language. Comprehension, activities and exercises in each chapter encourage students to explore texts in depth and create their own texts. Also, there are special chapters that focus on developing language skills through the use of texts.

Stimulus pictures and activities are in full colour and have been carefully chosen to ensure students find their encounters with texts both enjoyable and enduring. It is hoped they will feel motivated to explore and reach further into the world of texts.

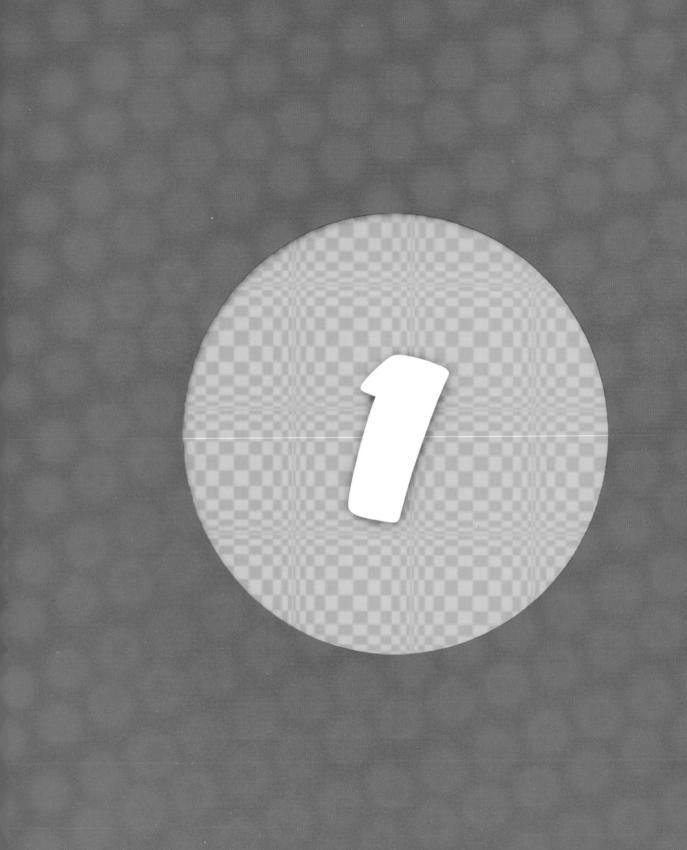

CHAPTER 1

TEXTS

WHAT YOU WILL LEARN IN THIS CHAPTER

• How to identify texts

HOW YOU WILL LEARN

• Reading different types of texts
• Recording your responses to the texts
• Writing your own texts

INTRODUCING TEXTS

WHAT ARE TEXTS?

Texts are the ways that we use language in speech and in writing. Jokes, poems, invitations, advertisements, novels and film scripts are examples of texts. Texts can be divided into two main groups: literary texts and factual texts.

LITERARY TEXTS

Literary texts include novels, plays and poems. They are works of fiction that allow us to experience new ways of viewing our world. They may help us to explore different emotions or think about something that is important. Some texts are designed to entertain us and make us laugh. Because literary texts have different purposes, they shape words in clearly identifiable patterns. It is usually very easy to tell the difference between a poem and a novel extract, for example, by simply looking at the pattern of words on the page.

There are three categories of literary texts.

I NARRATIVE TEXTS

Narrative texts include novels, short stories, fairytales, legends, myths and fables. They each have their own language pattern.

2 POETRY TEXTS

Poetry texts include odes, sonnets, free-verse forms, song lyrics, ballads and limericks.

3 DRAMA TEXTS

Drama texts include scripts for plays, television and radio dramas.

Factual texts can be spoken or written. They provide information and ideas in order to inform, educate, express a point of view, or report on a specific event or issue. The way the language is shaped depends upon the purpose of the text. Factual text may be accompanied by illustrations or pictures that are linked to the content of the piece. Factual texts include information reports, reviews, instructions and explanations.

FACTUAL TEXTS

LITERARY TEXTS	FACTUAL TEXTS
CARTOONS	ADVERTISEMENTS
COMIC STRIPS	DIARIES
FAIRYTALES	DIRECTIONS
FILM SCRIPTS	EDITORIALS
LIMERICKS	LETTERS
MYTHS	INSTRUCTIONS
NOVELS	INTERVIEWS
PLAYS	NEWSPAPER ARTICLES
POEMS	RECIPES
SHORT STORIES	REPORTS
SOAP OPERAS	REVIEWS

In this chapter you will read examples of literary texts. You will notice how they differ from each other. Later you will study each type in detail.

LITERARY TEXTS

A POEM

NEW BEGINNINGS

Each chapter that is ending
Leads us to a new beginning.
The past that we are leaving
Means a future we are winning.

Each change that fills the present
Sets the stage for our tomorrow,
And how we meet each challenge
Helps determine joy or sorrow.

In every new beginning
Spirit plays a vital part.
We must approach tomorrow
With a strong and steady heart.

So as we turn the corner
Let's all apprehension shed
And fill our hearts with confidence
As we proceed ahead.

Bruce B. Wilmer

EXPLORING THE TEXT

1 Write down two lines in the poem that you liked and explain why you liked them.

2 What is the main message in this poem?

3 What is the purpose of the poem? Is it to give information, tell a story, encourage you, entertain you or something else?

4 The pattern of words in a poem is different to that in other texts. Do you agree? Explain your answer.

YOUR TURN

Write your own poem about doing something new. You can use one of these titles or make up your own:

- **The First Time**
- **Starting Out**
- **A New World**
- **Beginnings**
- **A Fresh Start**

A NOVEL

This extract is taken from the opening of Morris Gleitzman's novel *Blabber Mouth*. We meet the main character, Rowena, and learn about some of the difficulties she faces on her first day in a new school.

I'm so dumb.

I never thought I'd say that about myself, but after what I've just done I deserve it.

How could I have messed up my first day here so totally and completely?

Two hours ago, when I walked into this school for the first time, the sun was shining, the birds were singing and, apart from a knot in my guts the size of Tasmania, life was great.

Now here I am, locked in the stationery cupboard.

Just me, a pile of exam papers and what smells like one of last year's cheese and devon (pressed meat) sandwiches.

Cheer up exam papers, cheer up ancient sanger (sandwich), if you think you're unpopular, take a look at me.

I wish those teachers would stop shouting at me to unlock the door and come out. I don't want to come out. I want to sit here in the dark with my friend the sandwich.

Oh no, now Ms Dunning's trying to pick the lock with the staff-room knife. One of the other teachers is telling her not to cut herself. The principal's telling her not to damage the staff-room knife.

I hope she doesn't cut herself because she was really good to me this morning.

I was an Orange-to-Dubbo-phone-line-in-a-heap-sized bundle of nerves when I walked into that classroom this morning with everyone staring. Even though we've been in the district over a week, and I've seen several of the kids in the main street, they still stared.

I didn't blame them. In small country towns you don't get much to stare at. Just newcomers and old men who dribble, mostly.

Ms Dunning was great. She told everyone to remember their manners or she'd kick them in the bum, and everyone laughed. Then when she saw the letters me and Dad had photocopied she said it was the best idea she'd seen since microwave pizza, and gave me permission to hand them round.

I watched anxiously while all the kids read the letter. I was pretty pleased with it, but you can never tell how an audience is going to react.

'G'day', the letter said, 'my name's Rowena Batts and, as you've probably noticed by now, I can't speak. Don't worry, but, we can still be friends cause I can write, draw, point, nod, shake my head, screw up my nose and do sign language. I used to go to a special school but the government closed it down. The reason I can't speak is I was born with some bits missing from my throat. (It's OK, I don't leak.) Apart from that, I'm completely normal and my hobbies are reading, watching TV and driving my Dad's tractor. I hope we can be friends, yours sincerely, Rowena Batts.'

That letter took me about two hours to write last night, not counting the time I spent arguing with Dad about the spelling, so I was pleased that most people read it all the way through.

Some kids smiled.

Some laughed, but in a nice way.

A few nudged each other and gave me smirky looks.

From *Blabber Mouth* by Morris Gleitzman

EXPLORING THE TEXT

1 Where is this story taking place?

2 'I'm so dumb.' Why does Rowena say this about herself?

3 Do you think that Miss Dunning is a good teacher? Why?

4 What do you learn about Rowena in the letter?

5 How do the students react when they read it?

6 'It's OK, I don't leak.' What does this comment show about Rowena's attitude to her disability?

7 *Blabber Mouth* is an Australian story. Find four words or phrases in the extract that support this claim.

8 Novels and poems are different types of literary texts. Jot down two differences between them.

9 Compare a novel and a play. How are they different?

10 Based on your reading of the extract, what is the purpose of this novel? Is it to entertain, to educate or to make you think about something? Explain your choice.

• **Write a story about a student starting school.**

CHECKLIST

To make the story interesting for the reader:

✔ Describe the main character.

✔ Explain how he or she feels.

✔ Give the reactions of the other students and teachers.

✔ Describe the scene where the action takes place.

✔ You may set your story in Ireland, outside Ireland, or even in outer space if you like!

✔ Use your imagination to make the story come alive.

✔ Make sure your story has a clear beginning, middle and ending.

✔ The most interesting stories usually have a problem that the main character must overcome by the end.

Hint

To improve your grades, always read over your work and make all the necessary corrections before you hand it up to your teacher. Use your dictionary to check your spellings.

The following extract is taken from *The Shakespeare Stealer* by Gary Blackwood. The novel is set in Elizabethan times and Widge, the hero, is an orphan who works for Dr Bright. In this scene, Widge learns that he is to leave Dr Bright and work for a new master. Dr Bright hands him over to the stranger for a large sum of money.

THE SHAKESPEARE STEALER

The stranger drew out a leather pouch and shook ten gold sovereigns from it onto the table. As he bent nearer the light of the pitch pot, I caught my first glimpse of his features. Dark, heavy brows met at the bridge of a long, hooked nose. On his left cheek, an ugly raised scar ran all the way from the corner of his eye into the depths of his dark beard. I must have gasped at the sight of it, for he turned toward me, throwing his face into shadow again.

He thrust the signed paper into the wallet at his belt, revealing for an instant the ornate handle of his rapier. 'If you have anything to take along, you'd best fetch it now, boy.'

It took even less time to gather up my belongings than it had for my life to be signed away. All I owned was the small dagger I used for eating, a linen tunic and woollen stockings I wore only on the Sabbath; a worn leather wallet containing money received each year on the anniversary of my birth – or as near it as could be determined; and an ill-fitting sheepskin doublet handed down from Dr Bright's son. It was little enough to show for fourteen years on this Earth.

Yet, all in all, I was more fortunate than many of my fellow orphans. Those who were unsound of mind or body were still at the orphanage. Others had died there.

I tied up my possessions with a length of cord and returned to where the men waited. Dr Bright fidgeted with the sovereigns, as though worried that they might be taken back. The stranger stood as still and silent as a figure carved of wood.

When he moved, it was to take me roughly by the arm and usher me toward the door. 'Keep a close eye on him, now,' the doctor called after us. I thought it was his way of expressing concern for my welfare. Then he added, 'He can be sluggish if you don't stir him from time to time with a stick.'

The stranger pushed me out the front door and closed it behind him. A thin rain had begun to fall. I hunched my shoulders against it and looked about for a wagon or carriage. There was none, only a single horse at the snubbing post. The stranger untied the animal and swung into the saddle. 'I've only the one mount. You'll have to walk.' He pulled the horse's head about and started off down the road.

I lingered a moment and turned to look back at the rectory. The windows were lighted now against the gathering dark. I half hoped someone from the household might be watching my departure, and might wish me Godspeed, and I could bid farewell in return before I left this place behind forever. There was no one, only the placid tabby cat gazing at me from under the shelter of the eaves.

'God buy you, then,' I told the cat and, slinging my bundle over my shoulder, turned and hurried off after my new master.

Extract from *The Shakespeare Stealer* by Gary Blackwood, The O'Brien Press Ltd.

EXPLORING THE TEXT

1 How old is Widge when he leaves the Bright household?

2 Apart from the clothes he is wearing, what else does he own? What does this tell the reader about him?

3 What happened to the other orphans at that time?

4 Why does Dr Bright want him to leave quickly?

5 Based on your reading of this extract, do you think that Dr Bright liked Widge? Explain your answer.

6 What is your opinion of the stranger?

7 Imagine you are Widge. What are your feelings as you leave Dr Bright's house and follow the stranger into the night?

8 This scene takes place early in the novel. Would you read on to find out what happened? Why?

9 Which of the two novel extracts do you prefer? Give reasons for your answer.

10 In groups of four, discuss the novels you have read. Make a list of the four favourite novels and briefly write down what they are about. Do not give away the endings! Now read your groups' list to the class. You may like to write the titles and the authors' names on a poster and put it on the wall.

YOUR TURN

- **Write a passage in which you describe two fictional characters meeting for the first time.**

CHECKLIST
Remember to:

✔ Describe the place where they meet.

✔ Describe the characters.

✔ Let the reader know why they are meeting.

✔ Include some conversation.

✔ Make something interesting happen.

A SHORT STORY

Here is a complete short story. It has a beginning, a middle and an ending. The entire story is told in a few pages.

HIS FIRST FLIGHT

The young seagull was alone on his ledge. His two brothers and his sister had already flown away the day before. He had been afraid to fly with them. Somehow when he had taken a little run forward to the brink of the ledge and attempted to flap his wings he became afraid. The great expanse of sea stretched down beneath, and it was such a long way down – miles down. He felt certain that his wings would never support him, so he bent his head and ran away back to the little hole under the ledge where he slept at night. Even when each of his brothers and his little sister, whose wings were far shorter than his own, ran to the brink, flapped their wings, and flew away, he failed to muster up courage to take the plunge which appeared to him so desperate. His father and mother had come around calling to him shrilly, upbraiding him, threatening to let him starve on his ledge unless he flew away. But for the life of him he could not move.

That was twenty-four hours ago. Since then nobody had come near him. The day before, all day long, he had watched his parents flying about with his brothers and sister, perfecting them in the art of flight, teaching them how to skim the waves and how to dive for fish. He had, in fact, seen his older brother catch his first herring and devour it, standing on a rock, while his parents circled around raising a proud cackle. And all the morning the whole family had walked about on the big plateau midway down the opposite cliff, taunting him with his cowardice.

The sun was now ascending the sky, blazing warmly on his ledge that faced the south. He felt the heat because he had not eaten since the previous nightfall. Then he had found a dried piece of mackerel's tail at the far end of his ledge. Now there was not a single scrap of food left. He had searched every inch, rooting among the rough, dirt-caked straw nest where he and his brothers and sister had been hatched. He even gnawed at the dried pieces of spotted eggshell. It was like eating part of himself. He had then trotted back and forth from one end of the ledge to the other, his grey body the colour of the cliff, his long grey legs stepping daintily, trying to find some means of reaching his parents without having to fly. But on each side of him the ledge ended in a sheer fall of precipice, with the sea beneath. And between him and his parents there was a deep, wide chasm. Surely he could reach them without flying if he could only move northwards along the cliff face? But then on what could he walk? There was no ledge, and he was not a fly. And above him he could see nothing. The precipice was sheer, and the top of it was perhaps farther away than the sea beneath him.

He stepped slowly out to the brink of the ledge and, standing on one leg with the other hidden under his wing, he closed one eye, then the other, and pretended to be falling asleep. Still they took no notice of him. He saw his two brothers and his sister lying on the plateau dozing, with their heads sunk into their necks. His father was preening the feathers on his white back. Only his mother was looking at him. She was standing on a little high hump on the plateau, her white breast thrust forward. Now and again she tore at a piece of fish that lay at her feet, and then scraped each side of her beak on the rock. The sight of the food maddened him. How he loved to tear food that way, scraping his beak now and again to whet it! He uttered a low cackle. His mother cackled too, and looked over at him.

'Ga, ga, ga,' he cried, begging her to bring him over some food. 'Gaw-ool-ah,' she screamed back derisively. But he kept calling plaintively, and after a minute or so he uttered a joyful scream. His mother had picked up a piece of fish and was flying across to him with it. He leaned out eagerly, tapping the rock with his feet, trying to get nearer to her as she flew across. But when she was just opposite to him, abreast of the ledge, she halted, her legs hanging limp, her wings motionless, the piece of fish in her beak almost within reach of his beak. He waited a moment in surprise, wondering why she did not come nearer, and then, maddened by hunger, he dived at the fish. With a loud scream he fell outwards and downwards into space. His mother had swooped upwards. As he passed beneath her he heard the swish of her wings. Then a monstrous terror seized him and his heart stood still. He could hear nothing. But it only lasted a moment. The next moment he felt his wings spread outwards. The wind rushed against his breast feathers, then under his stomach and against his wings. He could feel the tips of his wings cutting through the air. He was not falling headlong now. He was soaring gradually downwards and outwards. He was no longer afraid. He just felt a bit dizzy. Then he flapped his wings once and he soared upwards. He uttered a joyous scream and

flapped them again. He soared higher. He raised his breast and banked against the wind. 'Ga, ga, ga. Ga, ga, ga. Gaw-ool-ah.' His mother swooped past him, her wings making a loud noise. He answered her with another scream. Then his father flew over him screaming. Then he saw his two brothers and sister flying around him, curveting and banking and soaring and diving.

Then he completely forgot that he had not always been able to fly, and commenced himself to dive and soar and curvet, shrieking shrilly.

He was near the sea now, flying straight over it, facing straight out over the ocean. He saw a vast green sea beneath him, with little ridges moving over it, and he turned his beak sideways and crowed amusedly. His parents and his brothers and sister had landed on this green floor in front of him. They were beckoning to him, calling shrilly. He dropped his legs to stand on the green sea. His legs sank into it. He screamed with fright and attempted to rise again, flapping his wings. But he was tired and weak with hunger and he could not rise, exhausted by the strange exercise. His feet sank into the green sea, and then his belly touched it and he sank no farther. He was floating on it. And around him his family was screaming, praising him, and their beaks were offering him scraps of dog-fish.

He had made his first flight.

Short Stories of Liam O'Flaherty

Vocabulary

- muster up courage = to get up courage
- shrilly = very high, piercingly
- upbraiding = reproaching, speaking severely
- plateau = a flat area of high land
- taunting = jeering, teasing
- precipice = very steep place, cliff-face
- chasm = a wide gap
- derisively = scornfully
- plaintively = sadly
- curveting = moving sideways

EXPLORING THE TEXT

1 How many members are there in the family, including the young seagull?

2 Why will the seagull not fly? Is his fear understandable? Explain your answer.

3 How do his parents react when he stays on the ledge?

4 What does the young seagull do to pass the time?

5 Why is it important for him to fly?

6 How does his mother succeed in getting him to fly?

7 List the feelings of the young bird as he falls off the ledge.

8 How does his family show that they were pleased with him at the end?

9 What is the purpose of this story? Is it to entertain, to instruct, to make you think about how we react to doing something new, to make you remember doing something for the first time, or a mixture of all of these? Explain your answer.

10 In what way is a short story different from a novel?

YOUR TURN

- Tell the story from the mother's point of view. You could begin 'Yesterday I decided to teach my young chicks how to fly. It was more difficult than I expected . . . ' Remember to use the details given in 'His First Flight'. Do not change the story or the ending.

- Write your own short story based on the title 'The First Time Ever'. You may change the title to suit your story, if you wish.

For more information on short stories, turn to Chapter 2.

MODERN DRAMA

Going Home is a short play about Lee, a young child who is seriously ill. It is set in a hospital. While recovering from a major operation Lee has struck up a friendship with Tom Byrne, the hospital porter. In the final scene, Tom has come off duty and calls in to visit the sick child.

GOING HOME

A hospital ward lined with empty beds. One bed is occupied. A chair faces the occupied bed. Lee lies in the bed, staring at the ceiling. The porter, Tom Byrne, shuffles into the ward.

Byrne: Evening, Lee.

Lee (*voice very weak*): Hello, Tom.

Byrne: All alone I see. Everyone gone home, eh?

Lee: Yes, Tom.

Byrne: So you're the last patient in the ward. Well that's a good sign, isn't it? I mean if the others are cured and gone it won't be long until you're sent home also.

Long silence.

Byrne sits down on the chair and stretches his legs.

Lee: Tom?

Byrne: Yes, Lee.

Lee: You know a lot of things, don't you?

Byrne (*with a chuckle*): At my time of life a man knows more than what's good for him.

Lee: Can I ask you a question?

Byrne: Sure. Fire away.

Lee: What's heaven like?

Byrne: Heaven? Well I . . . I'm not sure. Why do you want to know?

Lee: Will there be other children there . . . my age?

Byrne (*cautiously*): I expect so.

Lee: And will I be able to play with them?

Byrne: What's all this about? You're not going to heaven for a long, long time. Not until you're years older than me.

Lee: It's just you see, since I've been sick, I haven't been allowed to play with other children in case I got an infection and I wondered if I would be able to play in heaven.

Byrne (*firmly*): Now no more of that, Lee. You're not going anywhere except home, like all the other children here.

Lee (*smiling*): It's all right, Tom, I'm not afraid of dying.

Byrne (*bewildered*): Why this dying business all of a sudden?

Lee: Last night my Nana came to me. She died last year. She told me it would not be long now and that she and Granddad were waiting.

Byrne (*gently*): Ah Lee, it was probably an hallucination, a dream. It's the medicine. Makes you imagine all sorts of things.

Lee shakes his head, then lies back against the pillows, exhausted.

Lee: It's okay. I don't mind. (*Wistfully*) Though sometimes I wish I was well enough to have a puppy – a little one, with big eyes and floppy ears. Daddy promised me one for my next birthday. (*Pause, and then quietly.*) I would have liked that.

Byrne: You'll have one, Lee. Sure you will.

Lee (*as if not hearing*): And a holiday. I would have liked to go on a holiday, just once. Maybe to the seaside. I never learned how to swim.

Silence.

Lee (*fainter*): Tom, will you tell them I love them?

Byrne: Who pet?

Lee: Mammy and Daddy.

Byrne: They'll be here soon. After tea. You can tell them then.

Lee (*urgently*): Promise me.

Byrne (*rising from the chair*): Of course but . . . .

Lee (*weaker*): I love you too.

Byrne (*sadly*): Lee, you'll be fine. It's the operation. You're feeling a little low, that's all. Why not have a rest now? Close your eyes. That's right.

Silence.

Tom Byrne looks down at the child, then pats the end of the bed and moves slowly towards the door. Lee's hand slides off the covers and hangs over the edge of the bed. Tom glances back and sees the arm dangling.

Byrne: Lee? Lee?

He hurries to the bedside. Oh my God!

He goes to the door. Nurse! Nurse! Quickly!

Exits

The lights fade.

The End.

EXPLORING THE TEXT

1 What is your opinion of Tom Byrne? Refer to the text in your answer.

2 How does Lee feel about death?

3 Do you think Tom accepts that Lee is dying? Why?

4 'Silences and pauses play an important part in this scene'. Do you agree with this statement? What do they indicate?

5 If you were directing this scene would you tell the actors to concentrate on their actions or on the tone of their voices? Give reasons for your answer.

6 Rehearse this scene with a classmate and present it to your class.

635491 2

University of Limerick

YOUR TURN

- **Write a short scene for a modern play. It can be humorous or sad. When you have finished you can perform your scene with your classmates. You may base the scene on one of the following if you wish:**
  - **friends meeting in a café**
  - **a team coach discussing a game with a player**
  - **a teacher and a student in a classroom situation**
  - **a parent confronting a child when the school report arrives home**
  - **a teenager asking permission to go to a disco**
  - **friends discussing a match**

CHECKLIST

✔ Remember to describe the setting, name the characters and give stage instructions.

✔ Place the characters name beside the lines he or she will deliver.

✔ The scene must hold the audience's attention. To make it interesting, something must happen. It must be dramatic. An exciting moment, a conflict, or an amusing or a tragic incident must be included.

RADIO DRAMA

Here is the script of a radio play based on Robert Louis Stevenson's *Treasure Island*. A mysterious seaman, known only as the Captain, has rented a room at the 'Admiral Benbow' Inn in Cornwall, in the eighteenth century. Young Jim Hawkins works there with his parents who own the inn. One cold, foggy afternoon a blind man with a stick approaches the inn from the road, looking for the Captain.

TREASURE ISLAND

Sound of seagulls crying and waves washing up the shore.

Visitor: Will any kind friend inform a poor blind man, who has lost the precious sight of his eyes in the gracious defence of his native country, England, and God bless King George! – where or in what part of this country he may now be?

Jim: You are at the 'Admiral Benbow', Black Hill Cove, my good man.

Visitor: I hear a voice, a young voice. Will you give me your hand, my kind young friend, and lead me in?

Jim: Take my hand.

Visitor: Now, boy, take me in to the captain.

Jim: Sir, upon my word I dare not.

Visitor: (*sneering*) Oh! That's it! Take me in straight or I'll break your arm.

Jim: (*a cry of pain*) Sir, it is for yourself I mean. The captain is not what he used to be. He sits with a drawn cutglass. Another gentleman . . .

Visitor: Come now, march.

Sound of footsteps on path and of door creaking open.

Visitor: (*sternly and then cruelly*) Lead me straight up to him, and when I'm in view, cry out, 'Here's a friend for you, Bill'. If you don't, I'll crack your arm.

Jim cries out in pain again.

Sound of parlour door opening.

Jim: (*repeats line shakily*) Here's a friend for you, Bill.

The Captain rises to his feet. Sound of chair legs scraping the wooden floor.

Visitor: (*threateningly*) Now Bill, sit where you are. If I can't see, I can

> hear a finger stirring. Business is business. Hold out your left hand. Boy, take his left hand by the wrist and bring it near to my right. Take this piece of paper, Bill. And now that's done. Goodbye.
>
> *Sound of stick tapping away into the distance. Sound of paper rustling.*
>
> **The Captain:** (*terrified*) It's the black spot! You know what this means, Jim? Six hours! I've only got another six hours! No, there's still time. We'll do them yet.
>
> *The Captain gives a sudden groan. Sound of chair falling over as he collapses onto the floor.*
>
> **Jim** (*frightened*) Captain! Captain! Help! Will somebody help? Mother, come quickly! He's dead! Oh no! He's dead!
>
> Robert Louis Stevenson

EXPLORING THE TEXT

1 Jot down the ways in which a radio script is like a play.

2 How is a radio script different from a play? You may refer to the script above in your answer.

3 Read this scene with two students in your class. How important is tone of voice?

- **Write your own radio script. You may use a scene from a story you know already or you can make up your own. Read it aloud with your friends, or record it and play it to your class. Remember to include some sound effects.**

CHECKLIST

✔ Place the characters name beside the lines he or she will deliver.

✔ Place instructions about the tone of voice beside the character's name.

✔ The scene must hold the audience's attention. To make it interesting, something must happen. It must be dramatic. An exciting moment, a conflict, or an amusing or a tragic incident must be included.

✔ Remember to include some sound effects.

CHAPTER 2

NARRATIVE FICTION: THE SHORT STORY

WHAT YOU WILL LEARN IN THIS CHAPTER

- How short stories are constructed

HOW YOU WILL LEARN

- Reading short stories and discussing them as a class or in groups
- Recording your responses to the short stories
- Writing your own short stories

INTRODUCING SHORT STORIES

People love stories. Stories are told to entertain and amuse, to explain and instruct. Stories are called narratives. A narrative is a spoken or written account of an event or a series of events and is recounted by a narrator. The narrator may be the writer, an observer, or one of the characters in the story.

A first person narrator tells the story from his or her point of view. He or she may be involved in the action and can give a good insight into the events as they occur. A first person narrator may be biased however and the reader knows only as much as the narrator at any moment in the narrative. The personal pronoun 'I' is used throughout the text in a first person narrative.

A third person narrator may not be involved in the story. Through a third person narrative, we can discover what all the characters are doing, learn what they are thinking and understand the motives for their actions. We may know more than the central character as a result. The personal pronouns 'he' and 'she' are used throughout the text in a third person narrative.

Short stories may be first or third person narratives. They have a beginning, a middle and an end and, unlike an extract, are not part of a longer narrative such as a novel. The best short stories concentrate on one important event and explore it in detail. The plot deals with a main event where a problem (complication) arises. The action normally occurs in a single place or setting over a short period of time. As a result, there are usually just two or three central characters and a few minor characters. Typically the climax of the story is found near the end.

INTRODUCTION (BEGINNING)

The introduction leads the reader into the story. It answers the questions who? what? where? and when?

COMPLICATION (MIDDLE)

The complication is the problem or difficulty the main character or characters experience and have to solve.

RESOLUTION (ENDING)

The resolution is the way the problem is solved. The story may have a happy or sad ending.

THE STRUCTURE OF A SHORT STORY

Title	What is the title? Does it catch your attention? How does it relate to the story?
Setting	When and where does the action take place? Is the setting important? Does it affect the way the characters behave?
Characters	How many main characters are there? Who are they? Are they true to life or are they exaggerated?
Plot	What is the story about? How does it hold your interest? How does the writer build up the suspense?
Narrator	Who is telling the story – the writer, an observer, a character involved in the action? Would the story be different if another character was the narrator?

FEATURES OF A SHORT STORY

Climax   What is the most dramatic part of the story? Where is the highest point or the lowest point for the main character? Where is it most exciting? Who is involved? Where is it found – near the beginning, the middle or at the end?

Resolution   Is there a surprise at the end? Are the difficulties solved? How are they solved? Is it a happy or a sad ending?

Read the passage below and see how many features of the short story you can find.

Title

THE TRUANT

Main characters

Michael Murphy sat outside the Principal's office, nervously fiddling with coins in his pocket. He felt uncomfortably hot, but was afraid to loosen his tie or take off his blazer.

Introduction

Ms Barton had very strict ideas about things like that and he was in enough trouble already.

It was unusually silent. The first class had started ten minutes earlier and the corridors were empty. In the distance, he could hear the shouts of lads training on the football pitch and their coach blowing his whistle. He wished he could be out there with them.

Setting

The door opened suddenly and the school secretary emerged, clutching a bundle of forms.

Other characters

'You may go in now,' she said coolly and swept past him. **Miss Prim-and-Proper-Prudy.** She always made him feel small, looking down her thin nose at him or raising her eyebrows over her spectacles when he raced through the main entrance fifteen minutes after the bell had rung.

'Late again,' she would say in an annoyingly superior tone.

Michael sighed and entered the carpeted room. Ms Barton was busy signing papers. She gestured to a seat. **Her fair hair was perfectly cut, her clothes well tailored. He became aware of how scruffy he looked.** Too late to do anything about it now.

Contrasting appearances

Ms Barton finished her work and placed her pen on the desk.

'How are you, Michael? You were absent yesterday.'

He cleared his throat.

'Er . . . fine, thanks. I had a twenty-four hour bug.'

Problem introduced

'Yet you were seen in town in the afternoon. How do you explain that?'

Complication

Her cold grey eyes seemed to bore right through him. His palms began to sweat. Where had he been spotted? Then it struck him. He had gone to the pub beside the girls' school. How could he have been so stupid? He might have known that someone would see him there. He thought quickly.

'Well, I went to the chemist for medicine you see, and then I had to go into *The Pony and Trap* because I felt sick.'

'You went into *The Pony and Trap* also?' her voice was icy. 'You were seen coming out of the games arcade.'

Reaction of main character

Problem gets worse

His face turned white. He'd totally forgotten the arcade. It had seemed like such a good idea at the time. The thought of nine classes in a row on a wet Monday in January had decided him. He had switched off the alarm clock and stayed in bed until noon, then headed into town for a few hours.

Ms Barton was droning on about his duties and responsibilities and how serious it was to miss school. She paused for a moment and then lowered her voice until it was dangerously quiet.

'This is your last warning. One more late morning, one more unexplained absence, one more excuse and you are out. Do I make myself clear?'

He nodded.

'If your poor mother were not in hospital, you would have been gone long ago. She has enough problems to cope with, without you adding to them. Now you had better return to your class. It is already 9.30.'

She turned to her computer screen.

Resolution

Emotional response

He stood up, feeling guilty, and made his way down the corridor. Who had reported him? Probably Prudy or maybe Barry Westen, the Maths teacher, who was always snooping around, trying to catch him doing something wrong. Michael felt a sudden surge of anger. He hated the place and everyone in it. As soon as the school year was over, he would walk out and never come back.

He came to 5G, flung open the classroom door angrily and marched to his desk. The students rose to their feet, scraping the chair legs on the polished floor.

'Good morning Mr Murphy,' they chorused.

● ● ● EXPLORING THE TEXT ● ● ●

1 What were your expectations when you read the title? Do you think the title is a suitable one? Give reasons for your answer.

2 Where is the story set?

3 How much time passes?

4 Briefly outline the plot in your own words.

5 How many characters are there in 'The Truant'? Who are they?

6 Who is the central character?

7 Would the story be different if Ms Prudy were the main character? Explain your answer.

8 Who is the narrator – an observer, the author, or a character in the story?

9 Where is the lowest point in the story for Michael?

10 What surprise is there at the end?

YOUR TURN

SCHOOL STORIES

Try writing your own imaginary story. You may like to use one of the following topics.

- **The day the class got out of control**

- **The day the students took over the school**

- **The day the school was taken over by aliens**

- **My perfect school**

- **The day I was sent to the school principal**

- **The day of the worst school excursion ever**

Here are some more short stories for you to read and enjoy.

THE TROUT

One of the first places Julia always ran to when they arrived in G—— was The Dark Walk. It is a laurel walk, very old; almost gone wild; a lofty midnight tunnel of smooth, sinewy branches. Underfoot the tough brown leaves are never dry enough to crackle: there is always a suggestion of damp and cool trickle.

She raced right into it. For the first few yards she always had the memory of the sun behind her, then she felt the dusk closing swiftly down on her so that she screamed with pleasure and raced on to reach the light at the far end; and it was always just a little too long in coming so that she emerged gasping, clasping her hands, laughing, drinking in the sun. When she was filled with the heat and glare, she would turn and consider the ordeal again.

This year she had the extra joy of showing it to her small brother, and of terrifying him as well as herself. And for him the fear lasted longer because his legs were so short and she had gone out at the far end while he was still screaming and racing.

When they had done this many times, they came back to the house to tell everybody that they had done it. He boasted. She mocked.

They squabbled.

'Cry babby!'

'You were afraid yourself, so there!'

'I won't take you any more.'

'You're a big pig.'

'I hate you.'

Tears were threatening, so somebody said, 'Did you see the well?' She opened her eyes at that and held up her long lovely neck suspiciously and decided to be incredulous. She was twelve and at that age little girls are beginning to suspect most stories: they have already found out too many, from Santa Claus to the stork. How could there be a well? In The Dark Walk? That she had visited year after year? Haughtily she said, 'Nonsense.'

But she went back, pretending to be going somewhere else, and she found a hole scooped in the rock at the side of the walk, choked with damp leaves, so shrouded by ferns that she uncovered it only after much searching. At the back of this little cavern there was about a quart of water. In the water she suddenly perceived a panting trout. She rushed for Stephen and dragged him to see, and they were both so excited that they were no longer afraid of the darkness as they hunched down and peered in at the fish panting in his tiny prison, his silver stomach going up and down like an engine.

Nobody knew how the trout got there. Even old Martin in the kitchen garden laughed and refused to believe that it was there, or pretended not to believe, until she forced him to come down and see. Kneeling and pushing back his tattered old cap he peered in.

'Be cripes, you're right. How the divil in hell did that fella get there?'

She stared at him suspiciously.

'You knew?' she accused; but he said, 'The divil a'know,' and reached down to lift it out. Convinced, she hauled him back. If she had found it, then it was her trout.

Her mother suggested that a bird had carried the spawn. Her father thought that in the winter a small streamlet might have carried it down there as a baby, and it had been safe until the summer came and the water began to dry up. She said, 'I see,' and went back to look again and consider the matter in private. Her brother remained behind, wanting to hear the whole story of the trout, not really interested in the actual trout but much interested in the story which his mummy began to make up for him on the lines, 'So one day Daddy Trout and Mammy Trout . . .' When he retailed it to her she said, 'Pooh!'

It troubled her that the trout was always in the same position; he had no room to turn; all the time the silver belly went up and down; otherwise he was motionless. She wondered what he ate, and in between visits to Joey Pony and the boat, and a bathe to get cool, she thought of his hunger. She brought him down bits of dough; once she brought him a worm. He ignored the food. He just went on panting. Hunched over him, she thought how all the winter, while she was at school, he had been in there. All the winter, in The Dark Walk, all day, all night, floating around alone. She drew the leaf of her hat down around her ears and chin and stared. She was still thinking of it as she lay in bed.

It was late June, the longest days of the year. The sun had sat still for a week, burning up the world. Although it was after ten o'clock, it was still bright and still hot. She lay on her back under a single sheet, with her long legs spread, trying to keep cool. She could see the D of the moon through the fir tree – they slept on the ground floor. Before they went to bed, her mummy had told Stephen the story of the trout again, and she, in her bed, had resolutely presented her back to them and read her book. But she had kept one ear cocked.

'And so, in the end, this naughty fish who would not stay at home got bigger and bigger and bigger, and the water got smaller and smaller. . . .'

Passionately she had whirled and cried, 'Mummy, don't make this a horrible old moral story!' Her mummy had brought in a fairy godmother then, who sent lots of rain, and filled the well, and a stream poured out and the trout floated away down to the river below. Staring at the moon she knew that there are no such things as fairy godmothers and that the trout, down in The Dark Walk, was panting like an engine. She heard somebody unwind a fishing reel. Would the *beasts* fish him out?

She sat up. Stephen was a hot lump of sleep, lazy thing. The Dark Walk would be full of little scraps of moon. She leaped up and looked out the window, and somehow it was not so lightsome now that she saw the dim mountains far away and the black firs against the breathing land and heard a dog say *bark-bark*. Quietly she lifted the ewer of water and climbed out the window and scuttled along the cool but cruel gravel down to the maw of the tunnel. Her pyjamas were very short, so that when she splashed water, it wet her ankles. She peered into the tunnel. Something alive rustled inside there. She raced in, and up and down she raced, and flurried, and cried aloud, 'Oh gosh, I can't find it,' and then at last she did. Kneeling down in the damp she put her hand into the slimy hole. When the body lashed, they were both mad with fright. But she gripped him and shoved him into the ewer and raced, with her teeth ground, out to the other end of the tunnel and down the steep paths to the river's edge.

All the time she could feel him lashing his tail against the side of the ewer. She was afraid he would jump right out. The gravel cut into her soles until she came to the cool ooze of the river's bank where the moon mice on the water crept into her feet. She poured out, watching until he plopped. For a second he was visible in the water. She hoped he was not dizzy. Then all she saw was the glimmer of the moon in the silent-flowing river, the dark firs, the dim mountains, and the radiant pointed face laughing down at her out of the empty sky.

She scuttled up the hill, in the window, plonked down the ewer, and flew through the air like a bird into bed. The dog said *bark-bark*. She heard the fishing reel whirring. She hugged herself and giggled. Like a river of joy, her holiday spread before her.

In the morning, Stephen rushed to her, shouting that 'he' was gone, and asking 'where' and 'how.' Lifting her nose in the air, she said superciliously, 'Fairy godmother, I suppose?' and strolled away, patting the palms of her hands.

The Finest Stories of Seán Ó Faoláin

Vocabulary

- lofty = high
- sinewy = strong
- ordeal = horrible experience
- incredulous = not believing
- motionless = without movement
- passionately = with great feeling
- ewer = jug
- superciliously = in a superior manner

●●●●● EXPLORING THE TEXT ●●●●●

1 Write a short paragraph outlining what happens at each of the following points in the story:
   – the introduction
   – the complication
   – the resolution

2 Do you think that this story has a good opening? Why or why not? Explain your answer.

3 Where is the climax (the point of greatest tension, the most exciting part of the story)?

4 What evidence is there to suggest that Julia is growing up?

5 In what ways are Julia and Stephen different?

6 What were Julia's reasons for rescuing the fish?

7 In your opinion, why did Julia not tell Stephen what really happened?

8 'She was twelve and at that age little girls are beginning to suspect most stories . . .' How many stories are referred to or told in this short story?

9 Is the author of 'The Trout' good at describing a scene? Refer to the text to support your answer.

10 This is a tale about two children, their parents, and a fish. It is also a story about the importance of the imagination in the lives of children. Do you agree? Explain your answer.

YOUR TURN

- Write a fairy story you would read to a five-year-old child. Do not tell a fairytale you already know. Make one up! Remember that the best fairytales begin 'Once upon time and a very long time ago . . .'

- Write out the dialogue (conversation) that takes place when Stephen tells his father that the fish has disappeared. It could begin like this:

  Stephen: 'Daddy, Daddy, the baby trout has gone!'

  Daddy: 'What baby trout?'

  Stephen: . . .

THE GREATEST

'Boys' group', said the teacher.

The second group of girls broke away from the centre of the dance studio, their faces flushed, their skin streaming with sweat.

A skinny girl, whose fair hair was scraped up into a bun, smiled at him, and pretended to collapse with exhaustion against the *barre*.

'Kevin, aren't you a boy any more?' asked the teacher.

'Oh yes!' he exclaimed. 'Sorry.'

He joined the other three boys in the class. They were waiting for him opposite the mirror.

'You've been in a dream today,' she said. 'Now I expect some nice high jumps from you boys, so we'll take it slower. That doesn't mean flat feet. I want to see those feet stretched. First position. And one and two.'

Kevin brought his arms up into first in front of him and out to the side to prepare for the jumps.

He loved the music the pianist chose for them. It made him feel as if he could leap as high and as powerfully as Mikhail Barishnikov. He knew that *barre* work was important but he liked the exercises in the centre of the studio best, especially when they had to leap.

But today all the spring had gone out of him. A lead weight seemed to pull him down. Bending his knees in a deep *plié* he thrust himself as high as he could into the air.

'I want to see the effort in your legs, not your faces,' remarked the teacher as he was in mid-spring.

They sprang in first position, their feet together, and out into second with their feet apart, then alternated from one to the other, out in, out in, sixteen times in each position, sixteen times for the change-overs.

'Don't collapse when you've finished,' said the teacher. 'Head up. Tummies in. And hold. Right everyone, back into the centre.'

It was the end of class. The girls made wide sweeping curtsies, the boys stepped to each side with the music and bowed.

'Thank you,' said the teacher.

They clapped to show their appreciation, as if they were in an adult class. Kevin knew that was what they did because in the holidays he was sometimes allowed to attend their Beginners' classes in ballet, even though he was only ten. He was more advanced than a beginner but at least the classes kept him fit.

Everyone ran to the corner of the studio to pick up their bags. It wasn't wise to leave any belongings in the changing-rooms. Too many things had been stolen from there.

The teacher stood by the door taking money from those who paid per class, or tickets from those whose parents paid for them ten at a time, which was cheaper.

Martin was standing in front of him, pouring out a handful of loose change into the teacher's tin. His father disapproved of boys or men doing ballet so Martin did it in secret and paid for his classes and fares by doing odd jobs. His only pair of dance tights were in ribbons and his dance shoes were so small that they hurt him.

Kevin handed his ticket to the teacher.

'I saw your father earlier on,' she said. 'Whose class is he taking?'

'He's not doing a class. It's an audition.'

'Is that why your head is full of cotton wool today? Worried for him?'

'Not exactly,' he said slowly.

He tugged at Martin's damp T-shirt.

'Dad gave me extra money today. I have to wait for him. Want some orange juice?'

'Yeah,' said Martin eagerly.

'Let's grab a table.'

They ran down the corridor to the canteen area and flung their bags on to chairs.

'I'm bushed,' said Martin.

'Were you sweeping up Mr Grotowsky's shop this morning?'

'Yeah. And I cleaned cars. Dad thinks I'm working this afternoon, too.'

'What if he checks up?'

'He won't. As long as he doesn't see me he doesn't care where I am.'

'Doesn't he wonder why you don't have any money when you go home?'

'No. I tell him I spend it on Wimpys or fruit machines.'

Although he was only eleven Martin had already decided what he wanted to do with his life. He had it all mapped out. First he'd be a dancer, then a choreographer. His idol was a tall thin black American teacher in the Big Studio. He had performed in and choreographed shows in the West End.

Professional dancers and students sweated and slaved for him, arching and stretching, moving in fast rhythms, leaping and spinning. There were black ones there too, like Martin. One day one of those black dancers would be him.

Some of the students were afraid of the teacher but they worked hard to be allowed to get into, and stay in, his classes.

'Get a classical training first,' he had told Martin abruptly when Martin had plucked up enough courage to ask his advice. So that's what Martin was doing.

'What's the audition for?' he asked.

'A musical.'

Kevin put their beakers of orange on the table.

'So what's the problem? Don't you think he has a chance?'

Kevin shrugged.

'Which one is it?'

'*Guys and Dolls*. He's going up for an acting part. He thinks his best chance of getting work as an actor is if he gets into a musical. He said no one will look at him if they know he's a dancer. He says directors think dancers haven't any brains.'

'I'd like to see them try a class.'

'Yes. That's what Dad says.'

'Is it because you're nervous for him? Is that it?'

'No. We had a row this morning. We just ended up shouting at one another. We didn't talk to each other all the way here. Even in the changing-room.'

'What was the row about?'

'About him auditioning for this job. I don't want him to get it.'

'Why? He's been going to enough voice classes.'

'Yes, I know,' he mumbled.

For the last year his father had been doing voice exercises every morning, taking singing lessons, working on scenes from plays at the Actors' Centre, practising audition speeches and songs, and reading plays.

'I didn't think he'd have to go away, though. This theatre's a repertory theatre and it's miles away. I'd only see him at the weekend. And even then it'd probably only be Sundays. And if he got it he'd start rehearsing two weeks after I start school.'

'So? You've been there before. Not like me. I start at the Comprehensive in a week's time. It'll be back to Saturday classes only.' He swallowed the last dregs of his orange juice.

'Want another? Dad said it was OK.'

'Yeah. I'll go and get them.'

Kevin handed him the money and pulled on his track-suit top over his T-shirt even though he was still boiling from the class.

He couldn't imagine his father being an actor. But his father had explained that he couldn't be a dancer all his life, that choreographers would eventually turn him down for younger dancers and, in fact, had already done so a couple of times. He had to decide which direction he wanted to go in before that started to become a habit.

For the last two years, since Kevin's mother had died, his father had only accepted work in cabaret in London, or bit parts in films, or had given dance classes. Otherwise he had been on the dole. Kevin was used to him being around now.

When his mother was alive and his parents were touring with a dance company, Kevin used to stay with a friend of the family. Dad said it would be like old times staying with her again. Kevin didn't want it to be like old times. He wanted things to stay just as they were.

He pulled on his track-suit trousers, dumped his holdall on his chair and waved to Martin.

'I'll be back in a minute,' he yelled.

He ran down the two flights of stairs which led to the entrance hall, past two of the studios there and downstairs to the basement where the changing-rooms and other studios were.

Outside the studio where the audition was taking place stood a crowd of people peering in at the windows. They were blocking the corridor so that dancers going to and from the changing-room had to keep pushing their way through with an urgent, 'Excuse me!'

The door to the studio opened and six disappointed men came out. Kevin's father wasn't among them.

Kevin squeezed in between two people by one of the windows and peered in.

Inside the steamed-up studio a group of men of every age, height and shape were listening to a woman director. A man was sitting at a piano.

The director was smiling and waving her arms about.

'Here. Squeeze in here,' said a dancer in a red leotard. 'You can see better.

They're auditioning for *Guys and Dolls*. It's the men's turn today.'

Kevin didn't let on that he knew.

'She's really putting them through it,' said the dancer.

'First they have to sing on their own and the MD, that's the man at the piano, decides who's going to stay. Then they have to learn a song together.'

'What's the song?' asked Kevin.

"Luck Be a Lady Tonight". Know it?'

Kevin nodded.

Know it? As soon as his father had heard he had been given the audition every song from *Guys and Dolls* had been played from breakfast to bedtime.

'Then they have to do an improvisation. The director chooses who to keep out of that lot and then the choreographer teaches them a dance routine.'

The dancing would be kid's stuff for his father, thought Kevin. He wiped the glass. His father was standing listening. So, he'd passed two singing tests. Now it was the acting.

The director was obviously explaining what the scene was about. She was pointing to individual men.

'She's telling them about the characters,' said the dancer.

Kevin felt angry. How could his father go through with it when he knew that Kevin didn't want him to go away? He observed his father's face, watched him grip his arms in front of himself and then quickly drop them and let out a breath.

'Excuse me!' he said fiercely, and he pushed himself out of the crowd and along the corridor to the stairs. And then he stopped. He remembered the look on his father's face and realised it was one of anxiety. It astounded him. He had seen his father upset before, but never scared. Why would he be scared? He was a brilliant dancer. But now, of course, he also needed to be a good actor. He was trying something new in front of actors who had been doing it for years and some of those actors were younger than him. That took guts, as Martin would say.

Kevin hadn't given a thought to how nervous his father might have been feeling. He knew how badly he missed the theatre. To start a new career when you were as old as him must be hard; harder too when he knew that Kevin hoped he would fail.

He turned and ran back down the corridor, ducked his head and pushed his way back into the crowd to where the dancer in the red leotard was standing. He wasn't too late. They hadn't started the improvisation yet. He stared through the glass willing his father to look at him.

The director stopped talking. The men began to move, their heads down in concentration as she backed away.

Please look this way, thought Kevin.

And then he did. He frowned and gazed sadly at him.

Kevin raised his thumb and mouthed, 'Good luck!'

At that his father's face burst into a smile.

'Thanks,' he mouthed back and he winked.

Kevin gave a wave and backed away through the crowd and along the corridor.

It was going to be all right, he thought. If his father did get the acting job he knew he'd be taken backstage and he'd meet lots of new people, and at least he wouldn't be touring so he could stay with him sometimes. And Martin could come too. And Dad would be happy again.

Martin wasn't at the table. Their bags were still there with the two plastic beakers of orange juice. Kevin knew where to find him. He walked to the corridor. Martin was gazing with admiration through one of the windows into the Big Studio. His idol was giving a class to the professional dancers.

He grinned when he saw Kevin.

'Guess what!' he squeaked. 'I was by the door when he went in and he noticed me. And he spoke to me. He looked at my shoes and said I ought to swap them for bigger ones at Lost Property and then, you know what he said? He said, 'Say I sent you!'

He turned back to watching the class and sighed.

'Isn't he the greatest?'

'Yes,' agreed Kevin, and he thought of his father. 'Yes, he's the greatest.'

Michelle Magorian

1 Who are the main characters? Are they true to life or are they exaggerated?

2 Where does the action take place? Is the setting important? Does it affect how the characters behave?

3 How do you know that Martin was determined to continue with his dance classes?

4 Why did Kevin's father audition for an acting part?

5 How did Kevin respond to his father's decision? Why did he feel this way? Did his attitude surprise you?

6 Describe how Kevin's father felt before his son wished him good luck and how he felt afterwards.

7 'Yes, he's the greatest.' What do you think that Kevin means by this?

8 At the end of the story, Kevin's opinion of his father has completely changed. Jot down the changes as they happened throughout the story.

9 What important issues were raised by the story? Refer to the text to support your answer.

10 Is this the type of story you would normally read? Did it make you think about some of your own attitudes? Would you recommend this story to your friends? Why or why not?

YOUR TURN

- Martin's father 'disapproved of boys and men doing ballet.' Do you agree or disagree with him. Why? Discuss your opinions with your class.

- Imagine you are Kevin. Write a letter to Martin's father to explain why his son should learn to dance. (For more information on letter writing, turn to Chapter 6)

- Do your own research (on the Internet or through a library) on the life of a famous dancer (e.g. ballet, disco, Irish or ballroom dancing). Write down your findings and present it to your class.

- Write a passage about someone you think is 'The Greatest'. It need not be a famous person.

CHARLES

The day my son Laurie started kindergarten, he gave up his little-boy clothes and began wearing blue jeans with a belt. I watched him go off that first morning with the older girl next door, looking as though he were going off to a fight.

He came home the same way at lunchtime. 'Isn't anybody here?' he yelled. At the table, he knocked over his little sister's milk.

'How was school today?' I asked. 'Did you learn anything?'

'I didn't learn nothing,' he said.

'Anything,' I said. 'Didn't learn anything.'

'But the teacher spanked a boy,' Laurie said, 'for being fresh.'

'What did he do?' I asked. 'Who was it?'

Laurie thought. 'It was Charles,' he said. 'The teacher spanked him and made him stand in the corner. He was really fresh.'

'What did he do?' I asked. But Laurie slid off his chair, took a cookie, and left.

The next day, Laurie remarked at lunch. 'Charles was bad again today.' He grinned. 'Today Charles hit the teacher,' he said.

'Good heavens,' I said. 'I suppose he got spanked again?'

'He sure did,' Laurie said.

'Why did Charles hit the teacher?' I asked. 'Because she tried to make him colour with red crayons. Charles wanted to colour with green crayons, so he hit the teacher. She spanked him and said nobody play with Charles, but everybody did.'

The third day, Charles bounced a seesaw onto the head of a little girl and made her bleed. The teacher made him stay inside during recess.

On Thursday, Charles had to stand in a corner, because he was pounding his feet on the floor during story time. Friday, Charles could not use the blackboard because he threw chalk.

On Saturday, I talked to my husband about it. 'Do you think kindergarten is too disturbing for Laurie?' I asked him. 'This Charles boy sounds like a bad influence.'

'It will be all right,' my husband said. 'There are bound to be people like Charles in the world. He might as well meet them now as later.'

On Monday, Laurie came home late. 'Charles!' he shouted, as he ran up to the house. 'Charles was bad again!'

I let him in and helped him to take off his coat. 'You know what Charles did?' he demanded. 'Charles yelled so much that the teacher came in from first grade. She said our teacher had to keep Charles quiet. And so Charles had to stay after school, and all the children stayed to watch him.'

'What did he do?' I asked.

'He just sat there,' Laurie said, noticing his father. 'Hi, Pop, you old dust mop.'

'What does this Charles look like?' my husband asked.

'What's his last name?'

'He's bigger than me,' Laurie said, 'and he doesn't wear a jacket.'

I could hardly wait for the first Parent-Teacher meeting. I wanted very much to meet Charles's mother. The meeting was still a week away.

On Tuesday, Laurie said, 'Our teacher had a friend come to see in school today.'

My husband and I said together, 'Was it Charles's mother?'

'Naah,' Laurie said. 'It was a man who came and made us do exercises, like this.' He humped off his chair and touched his toes. Then he sat down again. 'Charles didn't even do exercises.'

'Didn't he want to?' I asked.

'Naah,' Laurie said. 'Charles was so fresh to the teacher's friend, they wouldn't let him do exercises.'

'Fresh again?' I said.

'He kicked the teacher's friend,' Laurie said. 'The teacher's friend told Charles to touch his toes, and Charles kicked him.'

'What do you think they'll do about Charles?' my husband asked.

'I don't know,' Laurie said. 'Throw him out of school, I guess.'

Wednesday and Thursday were routine. Charles yelled during story time and hit a boy in the stomach and made him cry. On Friday, Charles stayed after school again, and so did all the other children.

On Monday of the third week, Laurie came home with another report. 'You know what Charles did today?' he demanded. 'He told a girl to say a word, and she said it. The teacher washed her mouth out with soap, and Charles laughed.'

'What word?' his father asked.

'It's so bad, I'll have to whisper it to you,' Laurie said and whispered into my husband's ear.

'Charles told the little girl to say that?' he said, his eyes widening.

'She said it twice,' Laurie said. 'Charles told her to say it twice.'

'What happened to Charles?' my husband asked.

'Nothing,' Laurie said. 'He was passing out the crayons.'

The next day, Charles said the evil word himself three or four times and got his mouth washed out with soap each time. He also threw chalk.

My husband came to the door that night as I was leaving for the Parent-Teacher meeting. 'Invite her over after the meeting,' he said. 'I want to get a look at the mother of that kid.'

'I hope she's there,' I said.

'She'll be there,' my husband said. 'How could they hold a Parent-Teacher meeting without Charles's mother?'

At the meeting, I looked over the faces of all the other mothers. None of them looked unhappy enough to be the mother of Charles. No one stood up and apologised for the way her son had been acting. No one mentioned Charles.

After the meeting, I found Laurie's teacher. 'I've been so anxious to meet you,' I said. 'I'm Laurie's mother.'

'Oh, yes,' she said. 'We're all so interested in Laurie.'

'He certainly likes kindergarten,' I said. 'He talks about it all the time.'

'He's had some trouble getting used to school,' she said, 'but he'll be all right.'

'Laurie usually adjusts quickly,' I said. 'I suppose his trouble might be from Charles's influence.'

'Charles?' the teacher said.

'Yes,' I said, laughing. 'You must have your hands full with Charles.'

'Charles?' she said. 'We don't have any Charles in the kindergarten.'

Shirley Jackson

EXPLORING THE TEXT

1 How does the title relate to the story?
2 What is your impression of Laurie's mother?
3 Describe the character of Laurie. How different is he from Charles?
4 How does the story hold your attention?
5 Who is the narrator? Why did the author not write the story from the point-of-view of the teacher?

6 What twist occurs at the end of 'Charles'?

7 The main character in the story is a young child. Do you think that this is a realistic (true-to-life) portrayal of a little boy? You might like to write about how he behaves at home and in school, how he speaks, etc.

8 In your opinion, why did Laurie behave the way he did?

9 How do you think the mother felt when she learnt that there was no child called 'Charles' in the kindergarten?

10 Did you enjoy reading this story? Why or why not?

YOUR TURN

- Write out the dialogue that takes place between the father and mother after the Parent-Teacher meeting.

- Write a letter from Laurie's teacher to her best friend, telling her about the new student in her class.

- Bad behaviour by a small number of students can make life difficult for everyone. Write out five important rules that students should follow in class.

- Continue the short story so that the reader discovers what happens to Laurie when his mother comes home.

ALL SUMMER IN A DAY

'Ready?'

'Ready.'

'Now?'

'Soon.'

'Do the scientists really know? Will it happen today, will it?'

'Look, look; see for yourself!'

The children pressed to each other like so many roses, so many weeds, intermixed, anxiously peering out for a look at the hidden sun.

It rained.

It had been raining for seven years; thousands upon thousands of days compounded and filled from one end to the other with rain, with the drum and gush of water, with the sweet crystal fall of showers and the concussion of storms so heavy they were tidal waves come over the islands. A thousand forests had been crushed under the rain and grown up a thousand times to be crushed again. This was the way life was forever on the planet Venus, and this was the schoolroom of the children of the rocket men and women who had come to a raining world to set up civilisation and live out their lives.

'It's stopping! It's stopping!'

'Yes, yes!'

Margot stood apart from them, from these children who could never remember a time when there wasn't rain and rain and rain. They were all nine years old, and, if there had been a day, seven years ago, when the sun came out for an hour and showed its face to the stunned world, they could not recall. Sometimes at night she heard them stir, in remembrance, and she knew they were dreaming and remembering gold or a yellow crayon or a coin large enough to buy the world with. She knew they thought they remembered a warmness, like a blushing in the face, in the body, in the arms and legs and trembling hands. Then they always awoke to the tatting drum, the endless shaking down of clear bead necklaces upon the roof, the walk, the gardens, the forests, and their dreams are gone.

All day yesterday they had read in class about the sun. About how like a lemon it was, and how hot. And they had written small stories or essays or poems about it:

> *I think the sun is a flower,*
> *That blooms for just one hour.*

That was Margot's poem, read in a quiet voice and in the still classroom while the rain was falling outside.

'Aw, you didn't write that!' protested one of the boys.

'I did,' said Margot. 'I did.'

'William!' said the teacher.

That was yesterday. Now the rain was slackening, and the children were crushed before the great thick windows.

'Where's teacher?'

'She'll be back.'

'She'd better hurry or we'll miss it!'

They turned on themselves, like a feverish wheel, all tumbling spokes.

Margot stood alone. She was a very frail girl who looked as if she had been lost in the rain for years and the rain had washed out the blue from her eyes and the red from her mouth and the yellow from her hair. She was an old photograph dusted from an album, whitened away, and if she spoke at all her

voice would be a ghost. Now she stood, separate, staring at the rain and the loud wet world beyond the huge glass.

'What're you looking at?' demanded William.

Margot said nothing.

'Speak when you're spoken to.' He gave her a shove. But she did not move; rather she let herself be moved only by him and nothing else.

They edged away from her; they would not look at her. She felt them go away. This was because she would play no games with them in the echoing tunnels of the underground city. If they tagged her and ran, she stood blinking after them and did not follow. When the class sang songs about happiness and life and games, her lips barely moved. Only when they sang about the sun and the summer did her lips move as she watched the drenched windows.

Then of course, the biggest crime of all was that she had come here only five years ago from Earth, and she remembered the sun and the way the sun was and the sky was when she was four in Ohio. And they, they had been on Venus all their lives, and they had been only two years old when last the sun came out and had long since forgotten the colour and heat of it and the way it really was. But Margot remembered.

'It's like a penny,' she said once, eyes closed.

'No, it's not!' the children cried.

'It's like a fire,' she said, 'in the stove.'

'You're lying, you don't remember!' cried the children.

But she remembered and stood quietly apart from all of them and watched the patterning windows. And once, a month ago, she had refused to shower in the school shower rooms, and clutched her hands to her ears and over her head, screaming the water mustn't touch her head. So after that, dimly, dimly, she sensed it, she was different, and they knew her difference and kept away.

There was talk that her father and mother were taking her back to Earth next year; it seemed vital to her that they do so, though it would mean the loss of thousands of dollars to her family. The children hated her for all these reason of big and little consequence. They hated her pale snow face, her waiting silence, her thinness, and possible future.

'Get away!' the boy gave her another push. 'What're you waiting for?'

Then, for the first time, she turned and looked at him. What she was waiting for was in her eyes.

'Well, don't wait around here!' cried the boy savagely. 'You won't see nothing!'

Her lips moved.

'Nothing!' he cried. 'It was all a joke, wasn't it?' He turned to the other children. 'Nothing's happening today. Is it?'

They all blinked at him and then, understanding, laughed and shook their heads. 'Nothing, nothing!'

'Oh, but,' Margot whispered, her eyes helpless. 'But this is the day, the scientists predict, they say, they know, the sun . . .'

'All a joke!' said the boy, and seized her roughly. 'Hey, everyone, let's put her in a closet before teacher comes!'

'No,' said Margot, falling back.

They surged about her, caught her up and bore her, protesting, and then pleading, and then crying, back into a tunnel, a room, a closet, where they slammed and locked the door marked closet. They stood looking at the door and saw it tremble from her beating and throwing herself against it. They heard her muffled cries. Then, smiling, they turned and went out and back down the tunnel to the classroom, just as the teacher arrived.

'Ready, children?' She glanced at her watch.

'Yes!' said everyone.

'Are we all here?'

'Yes!'

The rain slackened still more.

They crowded to the huge door.

The rain stopped.

It was as if, in the midst of a film concerning an avalanche, a tornado, a hurricane, a volcanic eruption, something had, first, gone wrong with the sound apparatus, thus muffling and finally cutting off all noise, all of the blasts and repercussions and thunders, and then, second, ripped the film from the projector and inserted in its place a peaceful tropical slide which did not move or tremble. The world ground to a standstill. The silence was so immense and unbelievable that you felt your ears had been stuffed or you had lost your hearing altogether. The children put their hands to their ears. They stood apart. The door slid back and the smell of the silent, waiting world came in to them.

The sun came out.

It was flaming bronze, and it was very large. The sky around it was a blazing blue tile colour. And the jungle burned with sunlight as the children, released from their spell, rushed out, yelling into the springtime.

'Now, don't go too far,' called the teacher after them. 'You've only two hours. You wouldn't want to get caught out!' But they were running and turning their faces up to the sky and feeling the sun on their cheeks like a warm iron; they were taking off their jackets and letting the sun burn their arms.

'Oh, it's better than the sun lamps.'

'Much, much better!'

They stopped running and stood in the great jungle that covered Venus, that grew and never stopped growing, tumultuously, even as you watched it. It was a nest of octopi, clustering up great arms of flesh-like weed, wavering, flowering in this brief spring. It was the colour of rubber and ash, this jungle, from the many years without sun. It was the colour of stones and white cheeses and ink, and it was the colour of the moon.

The children lay out, laughing, on the jungle mattress, and heard it sigh and squeak under them, resilient and alive. They ran among the trees, they slipped and fell, they pushed each other, they played hide-and-seek and tag, but most of all they squinted at the sun until tears ran down their faces. They put their hands up to that yellowness and that amazing blueness and they breathed of

fresh, fresh air and listened and listened to the silence that suspended them in a blessed sea of no sound and no motion. They looked at everything and savoured everything. Then wildly, like animals escaped from their caves, they ran and ran in shouting circles. They ran for an hour and did not stop running.

And then –

On the midst of their running one of the girls wailed.

Everyone stopped.

The girl, standing in the open, held out her hand.

'Oh, look, look,' she said, trembling.

They came slowly to look at her opened palm.

In the centre of it, cupped and huge, was a single raindrop.

She began to cry, looking at it.

They glanced quietly at the sky.

'Oh. Oh.'

A few cold drops fell on their noses and their cheeks and their mouths. The sun faded behind a stir of mist. A wind blew cool around them. They turned and started to walk back towards the underground house, their hands at their sides, their smiles vanishing away.

A boom of thunder startled them, and like leaves before a new hurricane, they tumbled upon each other and ran. Lightning struck ten miles away, five miles away, a mile, a half mile. The sky darkened into midnight in a flash.

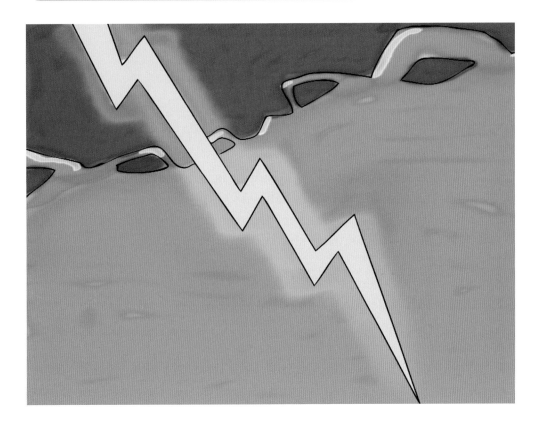

They stood in the doorway of the underground for a moment until it was raining hard. Then they closed the door and heard the gigantic sound of the rain falling in tons and avalanches, everywhere and forever.

'Will it be seven more years?'

'Yes. Seven.'

Then one of them gave a little cry.

'Margot!'

'What?'

'She's still in the closet where we locked her.'

'Margot.'

They stood as if someone had driven them, like so many stakes, into the floor. They looked at each other and then looked away. They glanced out at the world that was raining now and raining and raining steadily. They could not meet each other's glances. Their faces were solemn and pale. They looked at their hands and feet, their faces down.

'Margot.'

One of the girls said, 'Well . . .'

No one moved.

'Go on,' whispered the girl.

They walked slowly down the hall in the sound of cold rain. They turned through the doorway to the room in the sound of the storm and thunder, lightning on their faces, blue and terrible. They walked over to the closet door slowly and stood by it.

Behind the closet door was only silence. They unlocked the door, even more slowly, and let Margot out.

Ray Bradbury

EXPLORING THE TEXT

1 Where is the setting for this story? Is it important? How does it affect the way the students behave?

2 Who is the central character? Describe her appearance. Does her appearance suggest that she is happy or unhappy? Explain your answer.

3 Why do the others not like her?

4 How do they decide to punish her?

5 What does she do?

6 How do the students react to the sun?

7 When will the sun shine again? How does this affect their mood?

8 When the children realise that Margot is still locked in the closet,

how do they feel – sad, guilty, fearful, a mixture of these emotions? Refer to the text to support your answer.

9 'They unlocked the door, even more slowly, and let Margot out.' Write a paragraph telling what happened next.

10 This story examines some important themes and issues, such as bullying, revenge, jealousy and discrimination. In groups of two or three, pick out where each of the above is found in the text and underline it clearly. Within your group, choose one of the topics and discuss how it can affect a person. Write down your points and share them with your class.

YOUR TURN

- **Imagine you are a student in Margot's class. Write a diary entry describing the events of the day, including how the students treated Margot. Give your entry a date, which you write at the top of the page, for example, 1 July 6050.**

- **Write a speech persuading people not to discriminate against others. You may like to discuss how people discriminate against other people, their reasons for discriminating and the effects of discrimination. If you have experienced discrimination or seen it happen, you may refer to it in your speech also. You can deliver the speech to your class if you wish. A speech usually begins 'Good Morning/Afternoon everyone' and ends with 'Thank you.'**

- **Write a factual piece on one of the following:**
  - **The Solar System**
  - **Planet Earth**
  - **The Sun**
  - **Planet Venus**
  - **Rainforests**

  You can find information on the Internet, in a library or in your geography book.

FIRST CONFESSION

All the trouble began when my grandfather died and my grandmother – my father's mother – came to live with us. Relations in the one house are a strain at the best of times, but, to make matters worse, my grandmother was a real old countrywoman and quite unsuited to the life in town. She had a fat, wrinkled old face, and, to Mother's great indignation, went round the house in bare feet – the boots had her crippled, she said. For dinner she had a jug of porter and a pot of potatoes with – sometimes – a bit of salt fish, and she poured out the potatoes on the table and ate them slowly with great relish, using her fingers by way of a fork.

Now, girls are supposed to be fastidious, but I was the one who suffered most from this. Nora, my sister, just sucked up to the old woman for the penny she got every Friday out of the old-age pension, a thing I could not do. I was too honest, that was my trouble; and when I was playing with Bill Connell, the sergeant-major's son, and saw my grandmother steering up the path with the jug of porter sticking out from beneath her shawl, I was mortified. I made excuses not to let him come into the house, because I could never be sure what she would be up to when we went in.

When Mother was at work and my grandmother made the dinner I wouldn't touch it. Nora once tried to make me, but I hid under the table from her and took the bread-knife with me for protection. Nora let on to be very indignant (she wasn't, of course, but she knew Mother saw through her, so she sided with Gran) and came after me. I lashed out at her with the bread-knife, and after that she left me alone. I stayed there till Mother came in from work and made by dinner, but when Father came in later, Nora said in a shocked voice: 'Oh, Dadda, do you know what Jackie did at dinnertime?' then, of course, it all came out; Father gave me a flaking; Mother interfered, and for days after that he didn't speak to me and Mother barely spoke to Nora.

And all because of that old woman! God knows, I was heart-scalded.

Then, to crown my misfortunes, I had to make my first confession and communion. It was an old woman called Ryan who prepared us for these. She was about the one age with Gran; she was well-to-do, lived in a big house on Montenotte, wore a black cloak and bonnet, and came every day to school at three o'clock when we should have been going home, and talked to us of hell. She may have mentioned the other place as well, but that could only have been by accident, for hell had the first place in her heart.

She lit a candle, took out a new half-crown, and offered it to the first boy who would hold one finger – only one finger! – in the flame for five minutes by the school clock. Being always very ambitious I was tempted to volunteer, but I thought it might look greedy. Then she asked were we afraid of holding one finger – only one finger! – in a little candle flame for five minutes and not afraid of burning all over in roasting hot furnaces for all eternity. 'All eternity! Just think of that! Whole lifetime goes by and it's nothing, not even a drop in the ocean of your sufferings.' The woman was really interesting about hell, but my attention was all fixed on the half-crown. At the end of the lesson she put it back in her purse. It was a great disappointment; a religious woman like that, you wouldn't think she'd bother about a thing like a half-crown.

Another day she said she knew a priest who woke one night to find a fellow he didn't recognise leaning over the end of his bed. The priest was a bit frightened – naturally enough – but he asked the fellow what he wanted, and the fellow said in a deep, husky voice that he wanted to go to confession. The priest said it was an awkward time and wouldn't it do in the morning, but the fellow said that last time he went to confession, there was one sin he kept back, being ashamed to mention it, and now it was always on his mind. Then

the priest knew it was a bad case, because the fellow was after making a bad confession and committing a mortal sin. He got up to dress, and just then the cock crew in the yard outside, and – lo and behold! – when the priest looked round there was no sign of the fellow, only a smell of burning timber, and when the priest looked at his bed didn't he see the print of two hands burned in it? That was because the fellow had made a bad confession. This story made a shocking impression on me.

But the worst of all was when she showed us how to examine our conscience. Did we take the name of the Lord, our God, in vain? Did we honour our father and our mother? (I asked her did this include grandmothers and she said it did.) Did we love our neighbours as ourselves? Did we covet our neighbour's goods? (I thought of the way I felt about the penny that Nora got every Friday.) I decided that, between one thing and another, I must have broken the whole ten commandments, all on account of that old woman, and so far as I could see, so long as she remained in the house I had no hope of ever doing anything else.

I was scared to death of confession. The day the whole class went, I let on to have a toothache, hoping my absence wouldn't be noticed; but at three o'clock, just as I was feeling safe, along comes a chap with a message from Mrs Ryan that I was to go to confession myself on Saturday and be at the chapel for communion with the rest. To make it worse, Mother couldn't come with me and sent Nora instead.

Now, that girl had ways of tormenting me that Mother never knew of. She held my hand as we went down the hill, smiling sadly and saying how sorry she was for me, as if she were bringing me to the hospital for an operation.

'Oh, God help us!' she moaned. 'Isn't it a terrible pity you aren't a good boy? Oh, Jackie, my heart bleeds for you! How will you ever think of all your sins? Don't forget you have to tell him about the time you kicked Gran on the shin.'

'Lemme go!' I said, trying to drag myself free of her. 'I don't want to go to confession at all.'

'But sure, you'll have to go to confession, Jackie,' she replied in the same regretful tone. 'Sure, if you didn't, the parish priest would be up to the house, looking for you. Tisn't, God knows, that I'm not sorry for you. Do you remember the time you tried to kill me with the bread-knife under the table? And the language you used to me? I don't know what he'll do with you at all, Jackie. He might have to send you up to the bishop.'

I remember thinking bitterly that she didn't know the half of what I had to tell – if I told it. I knew I couldn't tell it, and understood perfectly why the fellow in Mrs Ryan's story made a bad confession; it seemed to me a great shame that people wouldn't stop criticising him. I remember that steep hill down to the church, and the sunlit hillsides beyond the valley of the river, which I saw in the gaps between the houses like Adam's last glimpse of Paradise.

Then, when she had manoeuvred me down the long flight of steps to the chapel yard, Nora suddenly changed her tone. She became the raging malicious devil she really was.

'There you are!' she said with a yelp of triumph, hurling me through the church door. 'And I hope he'll give you the penitential psalms, you dirty little caffler.'

I knew then I was lost, given up to eternal justice. The door with the coloured-glass panels swung shut behind me, the sunlight went out and gave place to deep shadow, and the wind whistled outside so that the silence within seemed to crackle like ice under my feet. Nora sat in front of me by the confession box. There were a couple of old women ahead of her, and then a miserable-looking poor devil came and wedged me in at the other side, so that I couldn't escape even if I had the courage. He joined his hands and rolled his eyes in the direction of the roof, muttering aspirations in an anguished tone, and I wondered had he a grandmother too. Only a grandmother could account for a fellow behaving in that heartbroken way, but he was better off than I, for he at least could go and confess his sins; while I would make a bad confession and then die in the night and be continually coming back and burning people's furniture.

Nora's turn came, and I heard the sound of something slamming, and then her voice as if butter wouldn't melt in her mouth, and then another slam, and out she came. God, the hypocrisy of women! Her eyes were lowered, her head was bowed, and her hands were joined very low down on her stomach, and she

walked up the aisle to the side altar looking like a saint. You never saw such an exhibition of devotion; and I remembered the devilish malice with which she had tormented me all the way from our door, and wondered were all religious people like that, really. It was my turn now. With the fear of damnation in my soul I went in, and the confessional door closed of itself behind me.

It was pitch-dark and I couldn't see priest or anything else. Then I really began to be frightened. In the darkness it was a matter between God and me, and He had all the odds. He knew what my intentions were before I even started; I had no chance. All I had ever been told about confession got mixed up in my mind, and I knelt to one wall and said: 'Bless me, father, for I have sinned; this is my first confession.' I waited for a few minutes, but nothing happened, so I tried it on the other wall. Nothing happened there either. He had me spotted all right.

It must have been then that I noticed the shelf at about one height with my head. It was really a place for grown-up people to rest their elbows, but in my distracted state I thought it was probably the place you were supposed to kneel. Of course, it was on the high side and not very deep, but I was always good at climbing and managed to get up all right. Staying up was the trouble. There was room only for my knees, and nothing you could get a grip on but a sort of wooden moulding a bit above it. I held on to the moulding and repeated the words a little louder, and this time something happened all right. A slide was slammed back; a little light entered the box, and a man's voice said:

'Who's there?'

"Tis me, father,' I said for fear he mightn't see me and go away again. I couldn't see him at all. The place the voice came from was under the moulding, about level with my knees, so I took a good grip of the moulding and swung myself down till I saw the astonished of a young priest looking up at me. He had to put his head on one side to see me, and I had to put mine on one side to see him, so we were more or less talking to one another upside-down. It struck me as a queer way of hearing confessions, but I didn't feel it my place to criticise.

'Bless me, father, for I have sinned; this is my first confession,' I rattled off all in one breath, and swung myself down the least shade more to make it easier for him.

'What are you doing up there?' he shouted in an angry voice, and the strain the politeness was putting on my hold of the moulding, and the shock of being addressed in such an uncivil tone, were too much for me. I lost my grip, tumbled, and hit the door an unmerciful wallop before I found myself flat on my back in the middle of the aisle. The people who had been waiting stood up with their mouths open. The priest opened the door of the middle box and came out, pushing his biretta back from his forehead; he looked something terrible. Then Nora came scampering down the aisle.

'Oh, you dirty little caffler!' she said. 'I might have known you'd do it. I might have known you'd disgrace me. I can't leave you out of my sight for one minute.'

Before I could even get to my feet to defend myself she bent down and gave me a clip across the ear. This reminded me that I was so stunned I had even forgotten to cry, so that people might think I wasn't hurt at all, when in fact I was probably maimed for life. I gave a roar out of me.

'What's all this about?' the priest hissed, getting angrier than ever and pushing Nora off me. 'How dare you hit the child like that, you little vixen.'

'But I can't do my penance with him, father,' Nora cried, cocking an outraged eye up at him.

'Well, go and do it, or I'll give you some more to do,' he said, giving me a hand up. 'Was it coming to confession you were, my poor man?' he asked me.

"Twas, father,' said I with a sob.

'Oh,' he said respectfully, a big hefty fellow like you must have terrible sins. Is this your first?'

"Tis, father,' said I.

'Worse and worse,' he said gloomily. 'The crimes of a lifetime. I don't know will I get rid of you at all today. You'd better wait now till I'm finished with these old ones. You can see by the looks of them they haven't much to tell.'

'I will, father,' I said with something approaching joy.

The relief of it was really enormous. Nora stuck out her tongue at me from behind his back, but I couldn't even be bothered retorting. I knew from the very moment that man opened his mouth that he was intelligent above the ordinary. When I had time to think, I saw how right I was. It only stood to reason that a fellow confessing after seven years would have more to tell than people that went every week. The crimes of a lifetime, exactly as he said. It was only what he expected, and the rest was the cackle of old women and girls with their talk of hell, the bishop, and the penitential psalms. That was all they knew. I started to make my examination of conscience, and barring the one bad business of my grandmother, it didn't seem so bad.

The next time the priest steered me into the confession box himself and left the shutter back, the way I could see him get in and sit down at the further side of the grille from me.

'Well, now,' he said, 'what do they call you?'

'Jackie, father,' said I.

'And what's a-trouble to you, Jackie?'

'Father,' I said, feeling I might as well get it over while I had him in good humour. 'I had it all arranged to kill my grandmother.'

He seemed a bit shaken by that, all right, because he said nothing for quite a while.

'My goodness,' he said at last, 'that'd be a shocking thing to do. What put that into your head?'

'Father,' I said, feeling very sorry for myself, 'she's an awful woman.'

'Is she?' he asked. 'What way is she awful?'

'She takes porter, father,' I said, knowing well from the way mother talked of it that this was a mortal sin, and hoping it would make the priest take a more favourable view of my case.

'Oh, my!' he said, and I could see he was impressed.

'And snuff, father,' said I.

'That's a bad case, sure enough, Jackie,' he said.

'And she goes round in her bare feet, father,' I went on in a rush of self-pity, 'and she knows I don't like her, and she gives pennies to Nora and none to me, and my da sides with her and flakes me, and one night I was so heart-scalded I made up my mind I'd have to kill her.'

'And what would you do with the body?' he asked with great interest.

'I was thinking I could chop that up and carry it away in a barrow I have,' I said.

'Begor, Jackie,' he said, 'do you know you're a terrible child?'

'I know, father,' I said, for I was just thinking the same thing myself. 'I tried to kill Nora too with a bread-knife under the table, only I missed her.'

'Is that the little girl that was beating you just now?' he asked.

'"Tis, father.'

'Someone will go for her with a bread-knife one day, and he won't miss her,' he said rather cryptically. 'You must have great courage. Between ourselves, there's a lot of people I'd like to do the same to, but I'd never have the nerve. Hanging is an awful death?'

'Is it, father?' I asked with the deepest interest – I was always very keen on

hanging. 'did you ever see a fellow hanged?'

'Dozens of them,' he said solemnly. 'And they all died roaring.'

'Jay!' I said.

'Oh, a horrible death!' he said with great satisfaction. 'Lots of the fellows I saw killed their grandmothers too, but they all said 'twas never worth it.'

He had me there for a full ten minutes talking, and then walked out the chapel yard with me. I was genuinely sorry to part with him, because he was the most entertaining character I'd ever met in the religious line. Outside, after the shadow of the church, the sunlight was like the roaring of waves on a beach; it dazzled me; and when the frozen silence melted and I heard the screech of trams on the road, my heart soared. I knew now I wouldn't die in the night and come back, leaving marks on my mother's furniture. It would be a great worry to her, and the poor soul had enough.

Nora was sitting on the railing, waiting for me, and she put on a very sour puss when she saw the priest with me. She was mad jealous because a priest had never come out of the church with her.

'Well,' she asked coldly, after he left me, 'what did he give you?'

'Three Hail Marys,' I said.

'Three Hail Marys,' she repeated incredulously. 'You mustn't have told him anything.'

'I told him everything,' I said confidently.

'About Gran and all?'

'About Gran and all.'

(All she wanted was to be able to go home and say I'd made a bad confession.)

'Did you tell him you went for me with the bread-knife?' she asked with a frown.

'I did to be sure.'

'And he only gave you three Hail Marys?'

'That's all.'

She slowly got down from the railing with a baffled air. Clearly, this was beyond her. As we mounted the steps back to the main road, she looked at me suspiciously.

'What are you sucking?' she asked.

'Bullseyes.'

'Was it the priest gave them to you?'

'"Twas.'

'Lord God,' she wailed bitterly, 'some people have all the luck! 'Tis no advantage to anybody trying to be good. I might just as well be a sinner like you.'

Frank O'Connor

EXPLORING THE TEXT

1 Name the characters in the introduction and give your impression of each of them.

2 'I was scared to death of confession.' Why is Jackie so afraid of confession?

3 What happens to him when he is in the confession box?

4 What was your opinion of the young priest at first? Did it change? Why or why not? Refer to the text to support your answer.

5 What is Nora's response to his penance?

6 Describe Jackie's character.

7 Did you find the resolution (ending) of this story satisfying? Explain why you liked or disliked it and refer to the text in your answer.

8 Jackie describes Nora as a 'raging malicious devil'. What evidence is there in the text to support this point of view? Refer to the whole story in your answer.

9 Humour plays an important role in this story. How did the writer create the humour in 'First Confession'? You may like to discuss the way the characters act, the things they say, the way they feel and the use of exaggeration.

10 Did this story hold your attention all the way through? In your answer refer to the plot (story-line), the characters and the use of humour.

YOUR TURN

- Imagine you are Nora. Write down your version of what happened the day you took Jackie to the church.

- Write a true account of a major public event in your life. It could be a wedding you attended, an important religious event or a funeral and so on.

- Draw a picture of the each of the main characters in the 'First Confession', as you imagine them. You can cut pictures from magazines, if you prefer. Consider what they look like, how they dress, what colours they wear. There are some details in the text to help you. Write the name of the character next to his or her picture.

- Choose a scene in the story, write it down as a short play and act it out with the help of your classmates. You will have to decide on who plays which part, what costumes to wear and what dialogue to use. (For more information on plays, turn to Chapter 11.)

LOVE LETTERS

My name's Nick and my chick's name's Fleur. And she has a friend called Helen who's got a boyfriend named Clive. Now this Clive is really weird. Well, he does one weird thing I know of anyway: he writes three-page letters to his girlfriend, Helen, every day.

'What's wrong with the nerd?' I asked Fleur. She'd spent a whole lunchtime telling me about him.

'There's nothing wrong with him,' she said. 'You're so unromantic, Nick.'

'Of course I'm not unromantic!' I said, and I offered her a lick of my ice-cream to prove it. She groaned and pulled her PE bag over her head. She didn't want to talk to me any more.

When girls go quiet, that's a bad sign!

'What's wrong?' I asked her.

'You don't love me,' she said.

'Of course I love you,' I told her. I offered her my whole ice-cream. She wouldn't take it.

'You don't love me *enough*,' she said.

'How much is *enough*?'

How much ice-cream did it take?

'You don't write me letters like Clive does to Helen,' she said.

'I don't need to, I see you every day in Computers,' I said. 'And Chemistry.'

'Clive sees Helen every day in Biology, and Textiles, and Home Science, and assembly, and roll call,' she said, 'and he writes letters to her!'

I knew what was happening here: my girlfriend was cooling on me.

'Okay,' I said, 'I'll write you a letter.'

'Aw Nick!' She whipped her PE bag off her head.

I was glad I'd weakened. Fleur is gorgeous. I couldn't risk losing her for the sake of a few lines scrawled on a piece of paper. I'm the envy of the boys' locker room, having her for a girlfriend.

I sat down that night and began my first letter: 'Dear Fleur. . .' then I stared at the page for the next half hour. What do you write in letters to someone you see every day? I chewed my pencil; I chewed my nails. Then, in desperation, I finally asked Mum.

'Write about the things you have in common,' Mum said, so I wrote the following: 'Wasn't that Computer class on Tuesday a roar? The best hit was when Brando tilted the computer to show us the little button underneath and the monitor fell off.'

I wrote about the Chemistry class too, though it wasn't quite as interesting. Not a single kid muffed their experiment and blew their eyebrows off. But then I got really creative at the end of the letter and added a postscript written in Basic.

I got the letter back next day with 'five-and-a-half out of twenty' marked on the bottom.

'What was wrong with it?' I asked Fleur.

'You made a lot of spelling mistakes for one thing,' she said.

'I was being myself!' I told her.

'I didn't notice, she said. 'You didn't say anything *personal* in it!'

Is that what she wanted, a *personal* letter?

I thought it over for five minutes. There were guys all round the lunch area just waiting to take my place and share their chocolate milk with the fabulous Fleur. If revealing a few personal secrets was what it took to keep her, I could do it.

'Dear Fleur. . .', I began the second letter that night. 'This is not something I'd tell everyone, but I use a deodorant. Only on sports day or in really hot weather of course.'

No, that was too personal. I ripped up the page and started again. 'Dear Fleur, Guess what? Mrs Hessell blew me up in History today for no reason at all. I was embarrassed to death. Goggle-eyes Gilda laughed her stupid head off.'

Actually, once I'd got started I found the personal stuff not that hard to write. I told Fleur what mark I'd really got in the English half-yearlies. Then I told her about a movie I'd seen where this pioneer farming guy loses his plough horse, then his wife, then his children, and then his cows get hoof rot. But even though he sits down and bawls his eyes out about it, in the end he walks off into the sunset, a stronger man.

'I'd like to suffer a great personal loss like that,' I told Fleur in the letter, 'and walk away stronger and nobler for it.'

Her sole comment on letter number two was: 'You didn't say anything in it about *me*.' And she went off to eat lunch with Helen.

It was time to hit the panic button. Fleur was drifting. I stuffed my sandwiches back in my bag and went looking for Clive. I bailed him up under the stairwell.

'Okay, what do you put in your letters to Helen?' I asked him.

Clive turned out to be a decent kid. He not only told me, he gave me a photocopy of the latest letter he was writing to Helen.

You should have seen it!

'Darling Helen, Your hair is like gold. Your eyes remind me of twilight reflected on Throsby Creek. Your ear lobes are... Your eyelashes are. . .' And so on. It was what you'd call a poetic autopsy.

And as if that wasn't bad enough, he then got into the declarations of love:

'You're special to me because . . . I yearn for you in History because . . . I can't eat noodles without thinking of you because . . .'

'Do girls really go for this sort of thing?' I asked him.

'Helen does,' he said. 'She'd drop me tomorrow if I stopped writing her letters. It's the price you pay if you want to keep your girlfriend.'

So I began my third letter, with Clive's photocopy propped up in front of me as a guide.

'Dear Fleur, Your hair is like. . .' I began.

Actually, I'd always thought that it was like fairy-floss, pretty from a distance but all gooey when you touched it – too much gel!

I scrapped that opening and started again.

'Dear Fleur, Your eyes are like. . .'

Actually they're a bit small and squinty. I think she might need glasses but she's not letting on.

Scrub the eyes.

'Dear Fleur, Your face is excellent overall. You look like one of those soap-opera dolls.'

I thought I would've been able to go on for hours about her face, but having said that, it seemed to sum her up.

I moved on to the declarations: 'I love you because. . .' I chewed my pencil again, then my fingernails. This time I couldn't ask Mum.

Why did I love Fleur? Because she was spunky. Because all the guys thought so too. Well, not all of them. Some of them thought she wasn't all that interesting to talk to, but I put that down to jealousy.

Still, I began to wonder, what had we talked about in the three weeks we'd been going out together? Not much really. She'd never been interested enough in my hockey playing to ask in-depth questions about it. And, I have to admit, I hadn't found her conversation on white ankle boots all that riveting either.

No wonder I was having so much trouble writing letters to her. We had nothing in common. I barely knew her. What were her views on nuclear waste disposal? Maybe she didn't have any. Was she for or against the death penalty? I didn't know.

I scrapped the letter, scrapped Clive's photocopy, and started again, this time with no trouble at all.

'Dear Fleur, This writing of letters was a very good idea because it gives me the opportunity to say something important to you. I think you're a nice girl and I've enjoyed going steady with you for three weeks but I think we should call it off. Even if it's a great personal loss to both of us. I'm sure we'll walk away stronger and nobler. Yours sincerely, Nick.'

I slipped the letter to her in Computers. She didn't take it too badly, just ripped it up and fed it through the shredder. But then two days later photocopies of my personal letter started to circulate the school.

I didn't mind though, because as a result of that, Goggle-eyes Gilda slipped me a note in History that said, briefly: 'I like your style, Nick. You've got depth.' I took another look at Goggle-eyes. I didn't mind her style either. She has this terrific laugh and she's a whizz on computers.

I wrote back straight away, my own kind of letter this time – honest and to the point: 'Dear Gilda, That three-minute talk you gave on speech day about Third World famine relief was really excellent. I'll be eating lunch in the quad if you'd care to join me.'

From *Changes and Other Stories* by Kate Walker

EXPLORING THE TEXT

1 Who is narrating the story? Who is his girlfriend?
2 Why does the narrator think that Clive is weird?
3 Why does Fleur think that Nick does not love her enough?
4 Why does Nick feel he has to write a second letter to Fleur?
5 What criticism does Fleur make of Nick's second letter?
6 Why did Nick have so much trouble writing letters to Fleur?
7 What was Fleur's response to Nick's last letter?
8 What do you think Gilda means by, 'You've got depth'?
9 Do you think Nick made a good choice in preferring Gilda to Fleur?
10 Do you think the ending is a good one? Why or why not?

YOUR TURN

WRITING A HUMOROUS LOVE LETTER

Using Clive's ideas, have some fun writing an imaginary love letter.

THE SCREAM

The playground at the end of the park is the usual sort of thing. A couple of swings, a slide, a ramp for roller skating, and an old climbing-frame with metal bars and tubes, quite good, actually, if you're young enough for it.

I hadn't been down there for ages, and it was only by chance that I went past it that day. I was on the way back from my friend's house, and I'd decided to do a detour round by the High Street and take a look at the new video releases.

It was a dull, cold day, and no one much was around. The playground was empty except for a bunch of kids, standing in a group in the far corner, away from the swings and slides, almost out of sight behind a tree.

I nearly walked right past them. It wasn't what they were saying that stopped me in my tracks. It was they way they sounded. Their voices were tense with excitement. Filled with violence.

Four boys, about nine or ten years old, were standing round a little kid, smaller than most of them, taunting him and jeering at him.

'Little scruff, aren't you, Paul?'

'Yeah, didn't you know, his mum gets all his clothes at the Oxfam shop.'

'No, she doesn't. She gets the stuff Oxfam won't take.'

The kid called Paul didn't look like much. His face was grey and strained. His eyes were darting about, looking for a way out of the tight ring that swayed round him. He must have thought a gap was opening up, because he made a jump towards it, but too slowly and hesitantly, as if he knew they'd stop him.

They did. One of them lunged forward and caught hold of his collar, pulling it away from the kid's scrawny little neck with one finger and thumb, and pretending to inspect it.

'Wah, look at this. Disgusting! He stinks! His mum never does any washing!'

'Nah, didn't you know, his mum likes him dirty. She's dirty herself. She washes his head down the toilet.'

'You ever been to his house?'

'Who, me? Course not. Might catch something.'

'They got things crawling out of their fridge.'

'They got green stuff growing on their walls.'

The kid's face was puckering up.

Don't cry! I thought. Whatever you do, don't cry! Say something cool. Walk away.

But he didn't. I never had.

'Get off me!' he wailed. 'It's not true! My house is much cleaner than yours. My clothes all come from Marks and Spencers. Look at the label if you don't believe me!' He was choking on his tears.

They moved in closer.

'Marks and Spencers! Yeah, sure.'

'It's true! Get off me! Leave me *alone*!'

They were pretending to stand loose and casual, but they were really as taut as guitar strings. They'd smelled blood.

'Leave you alone? We haven't touched you!'

'You starting something?'

'You want a fight, or what?'

None of them had seen me. I stood there helplessly, willing my thoughts across the tarmac, trying to get them into the kid's terrified brain.

Don't look so scared! I was silently shouting at him. Put your hands in your pockets. Shrug your shoulder. Smile. For heaven's sake, *smile*!

One of them flicked at the kid's shoulder as if he was brushing something off it, but the flick was as hard as a punch. The kid staggered backwards, and trod on the foot of a tall boy in a green jacket, who had been closing in behind him. The tall boy began to stamp about, faking agony, clutching at his foot.

'He stamped on my foot! Go on, Des, get him!'

My own heart was pounding now. My hands were clammy. I knew what was going to happen next.

I could go over and stop them, I told myself. They're only small. I could take them on easily. They had the smell of violence on them. I knew it. I feared and hated it. I didn't want to walk on, but my feet carried me away of their own accord.

The kid must have made some kind of desperate move, trying to pull away, or push through the circle or something, because I heard one of them shout, 'That's it, he pushed me! I'll do you for that!' and the others cheered him on.

'Yeah, go on, Des. Kill him!'

'Kick his head in!'

I was shaking.

He's got to learn, I remember thinking to myself. He's got to stand on his own two feet. But I knew the real reason that stopped me going in. I was scared of being marked out by them, scared of their dads and their big brothers, scared of them.

I tried not to hear the scuffling, scrabbling sound of their feet on the concrete, but I couldn't help hearing the kid scream. It wasn't the kind of scream that kids do deliberately, to attract attention and get an adult to rush on to the scene. It was a scream of pure loneliness and terror. It was the scream I'd felt time and gain, deep inside, the kind of scream that only dares to come out when all hope has gone.

I was already round the corner by the time I heard it, out on the main road. I stood still for a moment, not knowing what to do, feeling miserable, rotten and guilty.

The pavement was crowded. Women pushed past me, bumping their shopping bags into me.

People were picking over the racks outside the shoe shop, and gawping through the windows of the TV shop at twenty identical football games.

It's too late, anyway, I told myself. They'll have finished with him by now.

A bus pulled up at the stop just beside me. I don't know why I glanced along the upstairs windows. Habit, I suppose. I always used to have to check out the number 93 before I dared get on, in case Steve was on it. And it just so happened that he was. I stood, rooted to the pavement, and watched him.

When I was seeing him every day, before he was expelled from school, he'd always had at least one hanger-on with him, some little crawler who'd do whatever Steve said, and laugh whenever Steve tried to be funny, but he was on his own for once.

Perhaps I'd grown, or perhaps I'd always thought he was bigger than he really was. Anyway, he looked smaller now. He didn't see me at once. He was sitting hunched up, his face white and pinched.

I'd never noticed before that he was really quite thin. His shoulders were narrow and his arms looked puny. I flexed mine. I'd been working out a lot recently, and swimming twice a week. I felt good and strong.

Then he turned his head and looked right down at me. For a split second he actually looked pleased, as if he'd been lonely or something and was quite glad to see a face he knew. He almost smiled. At least, I think he did. I'd never seen him smile before, so I wasn't sure what it would look like.

He snapped out of it almost at once. He lunged his bullet head towards the window, baring his teeth and staring hard at me through narrowed eyes, his fingers jabbing the air obscenely. He looked like one of those vicious dogs that bark hysterically and strain to get at you when you walk past the place they think they're guarding.

Before, whenever I'd seen Steve, I'd pretended not to notice him. I'd always crossed the road, or turned to look in at a shop window, avoiding him as much as possible, getting out of his way as fast as I could. But quite suddenly, for the first time in my life, I wasn't afraid of him any more.

You're pathetic, I thought. Stupid. Alone. Out of the action. Out of my nightmares. No more screams for me.

I waved at him. His daft face dropped, and he gaped at me. Then, before he had time to get hold of himself, I turned round and began to dart back, down the side street, away from the main road, towards the playground.

I was strong. I was ready.

It seemed as if I'd been gone for hours, but actually it can't have been more than a minute or two.

They'd got the kid down on the ground, and he was feebly lashing out at them with his feet. He had his arms over his head and was trying to protect himself from the stabbing kicks of the smallest boy, whose body was so taut with anger I could almost feel it crackle, like electricity, from the other side of the playground.

'Beat him up, Des!' the other boys were shouting.

'Kick him hard!'

It was Des I would have to deal with.

They didn't hear me coming. I sprinted across the playground, grabbed Des by one shoulder and spun him round.

'Stop that. Stop it, you little . . .'

The other boys, concentrating on the kid on the ground, looked up, startled. One of them had been spitting on Paul's head. He wiped a slick of spittle off his chin. They began to back away, trying to resume their usual casual, swaggering posture. I only saw them out of the corner of my eye. I was watching Des.

He was sizing me up, turning an insolent shoulder towards me, balling his fists.

'Get off! Leave me alone! What's it got to do with you?'

The others saw him squaring up to me, took courage and came in nearer again. If Des went for me, they all would. If Des backed off, they'd all be too scared to touch me. It was only mental force that would drive them off, not violence. They wanted violence. They were good at it.

I looked Des up and down, pretending to recognise him.

'I know you. You beat up small kids all the time.'

He moved back a step.

'Nah. You don't know me. Never seen me.'

'Paul pushed him,' said one of the boys.

'He stamped on my foot,' said the boy in the green jacket. 'Asking for it.'

'Oh yeah?' I looked down at Paul. He wasn't even trying to get up off the ground. He'd covered his head with his jacket and his whole body was shaking with sobs. A cut on his hand was bleeding. 'Him? Asking for it. All of you against him?'

Two of them dropped their eyes and started kicking the toes of their trainers into the tarmac.

'Four against one? Think you're hard?'

'What's it to you? Who are you, anyway? What have I done?'

A whining note had crept into Des's voice. I didn't relax, but I felt more confident.

'I've been watching you,' I said, and found myself using Steve's old trick, staring close down into Des's eyes, moving my head gradually closer to his and forcing him to step back.

'My brother's going to get you,' he said, trying to bring the snarl back into his voice. 'He'll knife you.'

'Nobody's going to knife me.' I found to my surprise that I was enjoying myself. I bent down, pulled the jacket off Paul's head and dragged him to his feet. 'You're going to leave this kid alone, see? I'm going to make sure of that. You're going to be watched. You beat up anyone else and you'll be in trouble. Real trouble. Not just from me. You haven't seen my mates when they get angry. It's not a very nice thing to see.'

They were moving away step by step, cursing and threatening, their voices getting bolder and louder as the distance between us grew.

'I know you, Des,' I called after them. 'I know all of you. I've had a good look at you. Me and my friends'll be watching you.'

They didn't like that. They didn't like hearing me say Des's name. They speeded up. I heard their swearing get fainter as they went round the corner, and fade altogether into the roar of traffic on the High Street.

I turned back to Paul. He'd stopped crying. He was rubbing at his smeary nose with his sleeve.

'They done you before?'

He shook his head, not wanting to speak to me. I remembered exactly how he was feeling.

Humiliation. Hatred. Shame.

'They're nothing,' I said, trying to make him look up. 'They're pathetic. You're worth more than they are. You mustn't show them you're scared.'

'Leave me alone.' He was threatening to cry again. 'You don't know what it's like. You don't understand.'

I went over to one of the swings and sat down on it, letting it move me gently backwards and forwards.

'I do, as a matter of fact. It used to happen to me. Even in this playground once. A boy called Steve. Not any more, though. Never again.'

The clouds were beginning to lift. A group of mums and toddlers were coming into the playground. Paul turned away to hide his red eyes. The mums looked disapprovingly at me.

'It gets better,' I said, pushing the swing higher. 'Much better. You see through them in the end, see how stupid they are. You'll find that out one day. Anyway, they've done you over now, and they won't do it again. They'll leave you alone. If they don't they'll have me to . . .'

'Oi! Get down off that swing!

I looked round. I'd been talking to myself. Paul had gone, and in his place was the park-keeper, red-faced. I braked with my feet.

'Can't you read? No kids over fourteen allowed in this playground.'

'Where? I didn't see a notice.'

'Over there! By the gate!'

He was used to dealing with thugs like Steve and Des. He was working himself up, expecting trouble. I'd had enough for one day. I wasn't about to take him on.

I jumped off the swing and put my hands up.

'OK, OK!' I said. 'Don't shoot! I surrender!'

I walked past him, smiling at the row of frowning mums.

'And don't let me catch you in here again,' he shouted after me.

I went out of the playground and the gate swung shut behind me with a satisfying click. I felt extremely happy.

'Don't worry,' I said. 'I won't come back. Ever.'

Elizabeth Laird

1 In your opinion, why did the author set the story in a playground?

2 What attracts the narrator's attention to the boys?

3 What details does the author give about Paul? What do they tell you about the boy?

4 Describe the narrator's response to the scene. Did his reaction surprise you? Explain your answer.

5 The narrator gives his reasons for not helping Paul. Do you sympathise with him or do you think he should have helped?

6 The narrator later returns to the boy. Outline the series of events that led to this change of heart.

7 'They wanted violence. They were good at it.' Does their age excuse the actions of the bullies or make them seem worse? Why?

8 Based on your reading of the text, suggest reasons why Paul will not admit to being beaten up before.

9 Describe the character of the narrator. What was he like at the beginning of the story, how does he change and why, and what is he like at the end?

10 Coincidence plays an important role in this story. Trace the coincidences that occur throughout the text and comment on their significance.

YOUR TURN

- **In groups of four, describe the games you played as children in the playground.**

- **Write a short story that includes the line 'It was a scream of pure loneliness and terror.'**

> • **Imagine you are Paul. Write an account of what happened to you that day. Remember to describe how you felt.**

Writing stories and reading them to your class can be great fun. You may like to create your own book of short stories or collect one story from each student in your class and have a complete class collection.

Here are some titles, opening and closing lines to get you started.

- Help! Help!
- It was the worst idea ever.
- The lights flickered and went out. Suddenly . . .
- And where do you think you're going?
- A narrow escape
- You won't believe this, but . . .
- The Ghost of Crinkly Hall
- Tommy
- It's a dog's life.
- The footsteps came closer.
- The great beasts moved slowly through the forest.
- You've won!
- The china vase
- The small ring gleamed in the light.
- The space ship loomed in front of them, black and sinister.
- 'Let's dig!'
- The sun's rays slanted over the rooftops

CHECKLIST

✔ Remember to give your story a title.

✔ Describe the setting and the characters.

✔ Ensure it has a clear beginning, middle and end.

✔ Create a problem or challenge for the main character to solve.

✔ Put a twist at the end, if possible.

CHAPTER 3

PUNCTUATION MATTERS

WHAT YOU WILL LEARN IN THIS CHAPTER

- **How to punctuate sentences properly**
- **How to recognise a statement, an exclamation, or a question**

HOW YOU WILL LEARN

- **Reading sentences**
- **Punctuating examples**
- **Creating your own statements, exclamations and questions**

INTRODUCING SENTENCES

Private? No!

Punctuation can make a difference.

Private

No swimming

Allowed

does not mean the same as

Private?

No. Swimming

allowed.

Willard R. Espy

Properly punctuated work helps you to express yourself clearly. Willard R. Espy shows how the same words, written in the same order, can carry two different meanings when punctuation is added.

Poor punctuation can cause confusion, as this statement shows:

Sean bought coffee cakes and milk.

Does the writer mean that Sean bought cakes and milk, or does it mean that he bought coffee and cakes and milk? If Sean bought three types of goods, the sentence should read as follows:

Sean bought coffee, cakes and milk.

Sentences convey information. It is important to use them correctly.

A roadside sign in the Ox Mountains, designed to stop visitors hunting in the area, caused bewilderment to locals and foreigners alike. It read 'NO SHOOTING TOURISTS'.

Here are some definitions to assist you to write clearly.

A SENTENCE

A sentence is a collection of words that make sense. It can be a statement, an exclamation or a question.

A STATEMENT

A statement always begins with a capital letter and ends with a full stop.

Most teenagers enjoy listening to music.

AN EXCLAMATION

An exclamation begins with a capital letter and ends with an exclamation mark.

Look at that!

A QUESTION

A question begins with a capital letter and ends with a question mark.

Have you finished your homework?

CAPITAL LETTERS

A capital letter begins a sentence. It also is used to begin the names of people, places, films, books, TV shows and commercial products.

People	*Leonardo DiCaprio, Mother Teresa, Roald Dahl*
Places	*Rome, The Great Barrier Reef*
Products	*Nike, Mars Bar, Mercedes Benz*
Films and plays	*Romeo and Juliet, Titanic*
Books	*The Outsiders, Misery Guts*
TV shows	*'The Late Late Show', 'Fair City'*
Days, months, etc	*Wednesday, October, Easter, Christmas Day*

CAPITAL LETTERS AND FULL STOPS

A capital letter begins a sentence. A full stop is used to end a sentence. Make the meaning clear in each of these descriptions by adding capital letters and full stops.

THE MONSTER

I looked at the wretch the monster I had created glared back at me his jaws opened vague sounds came forth he lifted a withered hand horrified I rushed away now I am trembling downstairs (7 sentences)

From *Frankenstein* by Mary Shelley

WINTER

the night was bitterly cold snow lay heavily on the ground a hard, thick crust had formed in doorways and on fences the wind that howled abroad was savage it caught the snow and scattered it into the air (5 sentences)

From *Oliver Twist* by Charles Dickens

CAPITAL LETTERS IN EVERYDAY LIFE

Write down your favourite for each of the following. Make sure you use capital letters.

1 Your favourite film
2 Your favourite film actor
3 Your favourite song
4 Your favourite book
5 Your favourite city or town
6 A car you'd like to own
7 A book you've enjoyed reading
8 A sportsperson you like
9 A person in history whom you admire
10 Your favourite pop group

Punctuate the following statements, exclamations and questions.

1 the swan flew over the lake

2 who left the cage open

3 ireland is an island

4 would you like fish and chips for dinner

5 trains run on railway tracks

6 penguins live in the Antarctic

7 wasps can sting you

8 watch out

9 what would you do if you won the lottery

10 the golden eagle is almost extinct

Commas are frequently used to mark a natural pause in a sentence – the place where a person would naturally take a breath before reading on.

Commas help us to communicate clearly and accurately our written thoughts and ideas.

Flying down from the mountain, the eagle swooped low over the farm house.

Commas separate the name of the person spoken to, or addressed, from the rest of the sentence.

'Superman, what is your real identity?'

Commas are used to separate a series of adjectives describing a person. (Generally the comma is not inserted before the 'and'.)

Napoleon was cunning, aggressive, decisive and ruthless.

Commas separate items in a list.

The rock climber carried a rope, a helmet, a pack and a torch.

COMMAS

Commas are used after a phrase beginning a sentence.

By dawn, the bushfire was under control.

Commas are used to mark off an expression that explains.

The Blue Whale, the world's largest animal, can be seen cruising off the coast.

Commas are used to separate the parts of an address.

Her address is 10 Main Street, Newtown, Co. Dublin.

USING COMMAS

In each of the following sentences, supply a comma where a natural pause would occur.

1   On the tropical island many sea birds had built their nests.
2   While the snow fell the only thought in the skiers' minds was to keep warm.
3   Cheering wildly the spectators welcomed their favourite football team.
4   As the tide came in the fish began to leap.
5   The building began to collapse raising clouds of dust as it fell.
6   Unless we leave immediately we will miss the cruise.
7   Because a flood is coming everyone must leave the town.
8   Looking down through the plane's windows we saw the peaks of the Andes.

ADDING COMMAS

Write out the following sentences and correctly insert the missing commas.

1 A bird call halfway between a scream and a screech came from the bush.

2 Rome the capital of Italy is a very old city.

3 The campers carried food torches tents and sleeping bags.

4 My home is the Old Lighthouse Seal Rocks Co. Cork.

5 The old Aboriginal man was kind reliable brave and wise.

6 The refugees came from Vietnam Thailand Burma and Tibet.

7 The cheetah the world's fastest animal lives on the plains of Africa.

8 By sunset all the wheat had been harvested.

9 'Mr President are you ready to address the people now?'

10 'Spice Girls your act is on next.'

The apostrophe shows possession or ownership. Here are some basic guidelines for using the possessive form.

If the noun that possesses is singular, add 's.

the shark's teeth (the teeth of the shark)

If the noun that possesses is plural and already ends with s, simply add an apostrophe.

the girls' uniforms (the uniforms of the girls)

If the noun that possesses is plural but does not end with s, add 's.

the children's toys

THE APOSTROPHE

Change each of the following expressions so that an apostrophe is used to show ownership or possession. The first one has been done for you.

1 the playground of the school – the school's playground
2 the cars of the students
3 the noise of the trains
4 the food of the baby

5 the wings of the birds
6 the coats of the women
7 the crown of the queen
8 the roofs of the houses
9 the spire of the church
10 the bicycles of the ladies
11 the books of the children
12 the advice of the doctor

ADDING APOSTROPHES

In the following examples, the apostrophes have been left out. Correctly add the missing apostrophe to each of the following phrases.

1 the babies prams
2 the childrens library
3 tonights news
4 a planes wings
5 womens rights
6 a fathers warning
7 the mouses tail
8 mens shoes
9 Allisons books
10 the principals office

In speaking and in writing we often contract or shorten two words and use them as one word (an abbreviation). One use of the apostrophe is to indicate where letters have been left out.

She's leaving now. (She is leaving now.)

He couldn't drive. (He could not drive.)

'It's' is the short way of writing 'it is'. The apostrophe indicates that the 'i' has been dropped.

It's coming. (It is coming.)

SHORTENING OR ABBREVIATING WORDS

Abbreviate each of the following expressions by using an apostrophe.

1 It is best for him.
2 He could not move.
3 They have left.
4 We will get there.
5 She is the winner.
6 You are wrong.
7 I did not see it.
8 They cannot accept.

9   He was not there.
10 We will not be going.
11 What is the time?
12 I am ready.

FULL FORMS OF ABBREVIATIONS

Write down the full form of each of the following sentences.

1   I've finished.
2   You'd have won.
3   Where's the paper?
4   She'd like it.
5   Can't you hear?
6   He's absent.
7   I don't know.
8   We'll be there.
9   You've got it.
10 It's wonderful.
11 She couldn't hear.
12 Isn't he at school?

CHAPTER 4

NARRATIVE FICTION: NOVELS

WHAT YOU WILL LEARN IN THIS CHAPTER

- The structure of novels
- Features of the novel
- How authors describe characters and settings
- How to analyse front and back covers of novels

HOW YOU WILL LEARN

- Reading examples from novels
- Writing your own descriptions of people and settings
- Studying the covers of novels

INTRODUCING THE NOVEL

Novels are a form of narrative fiction, which means they tell a story. When we read a good novel, we enter an imaginary world and experience the emotions and lives of people in different places and at different times. Science fiction novels allow us to journey to distant galaxies in the future, while in historical novels we can roam the streets of the past. Crime fiction, fantasy, romance and adventure are some of the most popular types of novel today.

STRUCTURE OF A NOVEL
●●●●●

INTRODUCTION

In the introduction, we learn where and when the story is set, we meet the main characters and learn a little about their lives.

COMPLICATION

As we read on, we learn about the problems the characters experience.

RESOLUTION

The resolution is the end of the story. We find out whether or not the difficulties faced by the characters are solved. The ending may be happy or sad.

Plot	The plot is the story-line. It is the order in which events occur in the story.
Setting	The setting is the time and place where the action happens. Good descriptive writing helps us to imagine the places in the story.
Characters	The characters are those who take part in the story. They may be humans, animals, or imaginary beings.
Conflict	Conflict is a struggle or fight. It may occur between two characters, or two forces such as good and evil. Conflict may even occur within one of the characters in the novel, if he or she is torn between two courses of action. In this case, the character may know the

FEATURES OF THE NOVEL
●●●●●

right thing to do but is strongly tempted to do something wrong instead.

Suspense   Suspense is normally something very exciting or mysterious in a story. It adds to our enjoyment of the novel. The writer creates suspense so that we will read on to find out what happens next.

Theme   The theme is the central purpose of the novel. Authors may write simply to entertain us. They may write to make us think about a certain issue such as war, injustice or love. They may wish to challenge our attitudes towards others in society.

The three extracts that follow are examples of the introduction, complication and resolution in the novel *Jurassic Park*.

Jurassic Park was written by Michael Crichton. It tells the story of how dinosaurs were cloned and released in a theme park on a remote island. Unfortunately, everything went badly wrong and the dinosaurs escaped. Soon the lives of all those on the island were in danger.

A series of films, based on the novel, made millions of dollars and were seen by audiences around the world.

INTRODUCTION

This extract is taken from the introduction of the novel *Jurassic Park*. It appeared in one of the later films. A young girl is on holidays with her parents. She wanders off by herself and sees an unusual lizard. She thinks it would make a cute pet.

JURASSIC PARK

Tina ran until she was exhausted, and then she threw herself down on the sand and gleefully rolled to the water's edge. The ocean was warm, and there was hardly any surf at all. She sat for a while, catching her breath, and then she looked back toward her parents and the car, to see how far she had come.

Her mother waved, beckoning her to return. Tina waved back cheerfully, pretending she didn't understand. Tina didn't want to put sunscreen on. And she didn't want to go back and hear her mother talk about losing weight. She wanted to stay right here, and maybe see a sloth.

Tina had seen a sloth two days earlier at the zoo in San José. It looked like a Muppets' character, and it seemed harmless. In any case, it couldn't move fast, she could easily outrun it.

Now her mother was calling to her, and Tina decided to move out of the sun, back from the water, to the shade of the palm trees. In this part of the beach, the palm trees overhung a gnarled tangle of mangrove roots, which blocked any attempt to penetrate inland. Tina sat in the sand and kicked the dried mangrove leaves. She noticed many bird tracks in the sand. Costa Rica was famous for its birds. The guidebooks said there were three times as many birds in Costa Rica as in all of America and Canada.

In the sand, some of the three-toed bird tracks were small, and so faint they could hardly be seen. Other tracks were large, and cut deeper in the sand. Tina was looking idly at the tracks when she heard a chirping, followed by a rustling in the mangrove thicket.

Did sloths make a chirping sound? Tina didn't think so, but she wasn't sure. The chirping was probably some ocean bird. She waited quietly, not moving, hearing the rustling again, and finally she saw the source of the sounds. A few yards away, a lizard emerged from the mangrove roots and peered at her.

Tina held her breath. A new animal for her list! The lizard stood up on its hind legs, balancing on its thick tail, and stared at her. Standing like that, it was almost a foot tall, dark green with brown stripes along its back. Its tiny front

legs ended in little lizard fingers that wiggled in the air. The lizard cocked its head as it looked at her.

Tina thought it was cute. Sort of like a big salamander. She raised her hand and wiggled her fingers back.

The lizard wasn't frightened. It came toward her, walking upright on its hind legs. It was hardly bigger than a chicken, and like a chicken it bobbed its head as it walked. Tina thought it would make a wonderful pet.

She noticed that the lizard left three-toed tracks that looked exactly like bird tracks. The lizard came closer to Tina. She kept her body still, not wanting to frighten the little animal. She was amazed that it would come so close, but she remembered that this was a national park. All the animals in the park would know that they were protected. This lizard was probably tame. Maybe it even expected her to give it some food. Unfortunately she didn't have any. Slowly, Tina extended her hand, palm open, to show she didn't have any food.

The lizard paused, cocked his head, and chirped.

'Sorry,' Tina said. 'I just don't have anything.'

And then, without warning, the lizard jumped up onto her outstretched hand. Tina could feel its little toes pinching the skin of her palm, and she felt the surprising weight of the animal's body pressing her arm down.

And then the lizard scrambled up her arm, toward her face.

'I just wish I could see her,' Ellen Bowman said, squinting in the sunlight. 'That's all. Just see her.'

'I'm sure she's fine,' Mike said, picking through the box lunch packed by the hotel. There was unappetizing grilled chicken, and some kind of a meat-filled pastry. Not that Ellen would eat any of it.

'You don't think she'd leave the beach?' Ellen said.

'No, hon, I don't.'

'I feel so isolated here,' Ellen said.

'I thought that's what you wanted,' Mike Bowman said.

'I did.'

'Well, then, what's the problem?'

'I just wish I could see her, is all,' Ellen said.

Then, from down the beach, carried by the wind, they heard their daughter's voice. She was screaming.

EXPLORING THE TEXT

1 What is the setting in this extract? Why is it important?

2 Describe the animal that Tina discovers. Is there anything in its appearance to suggest that it is dangerous?

3 'Then, from down the beach, carried by the wind, they heard their daughter's voice. She was screaming.' Why did the author end the chapter at this point?

4 Would you continue to read the novel? Give reasons for your answer.

The main problem in the novel occurs when one of the workers turns off the electricity so that he can steal from the laboratories and make his escape afterwards. The electric fences are now useless, allowing the most dangerous dinosaurs to leave their enclosures. In the meantime, Tim and his sister Lex, the grandchildren of the park's owner, are stranded in a car within the park, because the cars are run on electricity. Ed Regis is the adult in charge of them. Two scientists, Dr Grant and Dr Malcolm are sitting in the Land Cruiser behind. They can talk to each other by radio. Suddenly Ed jumps out of the car and runs away. Tim looks up and sees an enormous dinosaur. Dr Grant tells them over the radio to stay in the car and keep very quiet.

COMPLICATION
●●●●●

JURASSIC PARK

'Okay,' Tim clicked the radio off. 'You hear that, Lex?'

His sister nodded, silently. She never took her eyes off the dinosaur. The tyrannosaur roared. In the glare of lightning, they saw it pull free of the fence and take a bounding step forward.

Now it was standing between the two cars. Tim couldn't see Dr Grant's car any more, because the huge body blocked his view. The rain ran in rivulets down the pebbled skin of the muscular hind legs. He couldn't see the animal's head, which was high above the roofline.

The tyrannosaur moved around the side of their car. It went to the very spot where Tim had gotten out of the car. Where Ed Regis had gotten out of the car. The animal paused here. The big head ducked down, toward the mud.

Tim looked back at Dr Grant and Dr Malcolm in the rear car. Their faces were tense as they stared forward through the windshield.

The huge head raised back up, jaws open, and then stopped by the side windows. In the glare of lightning, they saw the beady, expressionless reptile eye moving in the socket.

It was looking in the car.

His sister's breath came in ragged, frightened gasps. He reached out and

squeezed her arm, hoping she would stay quiet. The dinosaur continued to stare for a long time through the side window. Perhaps the dinosaur couldn't really see them, he thought. Finally the head lifted up, out of view again.

'Timmy . . .' Lex whispered.

'It's okay,' Tim whispered. 'I don't think it saw us.'

He was looking back toward Dr Grant when a jolting impact rocked the Land Cruiser and shattered the windshield in a spider-web as the tyrannosaur's head crashed against the hood of the Land Cruiser. Tim was knocked flat on the seat. The night-vision goggles slid off his forehead.

He got back up quickly, blinking in the darkness, his mouth warm with blood.

'Lex?'

He couldn't see his sister anywhere.

The tyrannosaur stood near the front of the Land Cruiser, its chest moving as it breathed, the forelimbs making clawing movements in the air.

'Lex!' Tim whispered. Then he heard her groan. She was lying somewhere on the floor under the front seat.

Then the huge head came down, entirely blocking the shattered windshield. The tyrannosaur banged again on the front hood of the Land Cruiser. Tim grabbed the seat as the car rocked on its wheels. The tyrannosaur banged down twice more, denting the metal.

Then it moved around the side of the car. The big raised tail blocked his view out of all the side windows. At the back, the animal snorted, a deep rumbling growl that blended with the thunder. It sank its jaws into the spare tire mounted on the back of the Land Cruiser and, in a single head shake, tore it away. The rear of the car lifted into the air for a moment, then it thumped down with a muddy splash.

Tim grabbed the radio. 'We're okay,' he said. There was a shrill metallic scrape as claws raked the roof of the car. Tim's heart was pounding in his chest. He couldn't see anything out of the windows on the right side except pebbled leathery flesh. The tyrannosaur was leaning against the car, which rocked back and forth with each breath, the springs and metal creaking loudly.

Lex groaned again. Tim put down the radio, and started to crawl over into the front seat. The tyrannosaur roared and the metal roof dented downward. Tim felt a sharp pain in his head and tumbled to the floor, onto the transmission hump. He found himself lying alongside Lex, and was shocked to see that the whole side of her head was covered in blood. She looked unconscious.

There was another jolting impact, and pieces of glass fell all around him. Tim felt rain. He looked up and saw that the front windshield had broken out. There was just a jagged rim of glass and, beyond, the big head of the dinosaur. *Looking down at him.*

Tim felt a sudden chill and then the head rushed forward toward him, the jaws open. There was the squeal of metal against teeth, and he felt the hot stinking breath of the animal and a thick tongue stuck into the car through the windshield opening. The tongue slapped wetly around inside the car – he felt the hot lather of dinosaur saliva – and the tyrannosaur roared – deafening sound inside the car –

The head pulled away abruptly.

Tim scrambled up, avoiding the dent in the roof. There was still room to sit on the front seat by the passenger door. The tyrannosaur stood in the rain near the front fender. It seemed confused by what had happened to it. Blood dripped freely from its jaws.

The tyrannosaur looked at Tim, cocking its head to stare with one big eye. The head moved close to the car, sideways, and peered in. blood spattered on the dented hood of the Land Cruiser, mixing with the rain.

It can't get to me, Tim thought. It's too big.

Then the head pulled away, and in the flare of lightning he saw the hind leg lift up. And the world tilted crazily as the Land Cruiser slammed over on its side, the window splatting in the mud. He saw Lex fall helplessly against the side window, and he fell down beside her, banging his head. Tim felt dizzy. Then the tyrannosaur's jaws clamped onto the window frame, and the whole Land Cruiser was lifted up into the air, and shaken.

'Timmy!' Lex shrieked, so near to his ear that it hurt. She was suddenly awake, and he grabbed her as the tyrannosaur crashed the car down again. Tim felt a stabbing pain in his side, and his sister fell on top of him. The car went up again, tilting crazily. Lex shouted '*Timmy!*' and he saw the door give way beneath her, and she fell out of the car into the mud, but Tim couldn't answer, because in the next instant everything swung crazily – he saw the trunks of the palm trees sliding downward past him – moving sideways through the air – he glimpsed the ground very far below – the hot roar of the tyrannosaur – the blazing eye – the tops of the palm trees –

And then, with a metallic scraping shriek, the car fell from the tyrannosaur's jaws, a sickening fall, and Tim's stomach heaved in the moment before the world became totally black, and silent.

EXPLORING THE TEXT

1 How does the author give a sense of the size of the dinosaur?
2 What evidence is there to suggest that the tyrannosaur is incredibly strong?
3 There is a real sense of fear in the extract. Do you agree? Refer to the text in your answer.
4 When you come to the end of the extract, would you want to read the rest of the chapter? Why or why not?

RESOLUTION

Having experienced hair-raising adventures and narrow escapes, Tim and Lex finally make it back to the main buildings on the island and get help for their friends, Ellie, Dr Grant and Gennaro. In the novel, the children are picked up by the rescuers and flown by helicopter to safety. In the meantime, the adults have arrived on a beach where they discover dinosaurs trying to leave the island.

JURASSIC PARK

'Migrating!' Ellie said. 'That's fantastic!'

'Yes,' Grant said. He was grinning.

Ellie said, 'Where do you suppose they want to go?'

'I don't know,' Grant said, and then the big helicopters burst through the fog, thundering and wheeling over the landscape, their underbellies heavy with armament. The raptors scattered in alarm as one of the helicopters circled back, following the line of the surf, and then moved in to land on the beach. A door was flung open and soldiers in olive uniforms came running toward

them. Grant heard the rapid babble of voices in Spanish and saw that Muldoon was already aboard with the kids. One of the soldiers said in English, 'Please, you will come with us. Please, there is no time here.'

Grant looked back at the beach where the raptors had been, but they were gone. All the animals had vanished. It was as if they had never existed. The soldiers were tugging at him, and he allowed himself to be led beneath the thumping blades and climbed up through the big door. Muldoon leaned over and shouted in Grant's ear, 'They want us out of here now. They're going to do it now!'

The soldiers pushed Grant and Ellie and Gennaro into seats, and helped them clip on the harnesses. Tim and Lex waved to him and he suddenly saw how young they were, and how exhausted. Lex was yawning, leaning against her brother's shoulder.

An officer came toward Grant and shouted, 'Señor: are you in charge?'

'No,' Grant said. 'I'm not in charge.'

'Who is in charge, please?'

'I don't know.'

The officer went on to Gennaro, and asked the same question: 'Are you in charge?'

'No,' Gennaro said.

The officer looked at Ellie, but said nothing to her. The door was left open as the helicopter lifted away from the beach, and Grant leaned out to see if he could catch a last look at the raptors, but then the helicopter was above the palm trees, moving north over the island.

Grant leaned to Muldoon, and shouted: 'What about the others?'

Muldoon shouted, 'They've already taken off Harding and some workmen. Hammond had an accident. Found him on the hill near his bungalow. Must have fallen.'

'Is he alright?' Grant said.

'No. Compys got him.'

'What about Malcolm?' Grant said.

Muldoon shook his head.

Grant was too tired to feel much of anything. He turned away, and looked back out the door. It was getting dark now, and in the fading light he could barely see the little rex, with bloody jaws, crouched over a hadrosaur by the edge of the lagoon and looking up at the helicopter and roaring as it passed by.

Somewhere behind them they heard explosions, and then ahead they saw another helicopter wheeling through the mist over the visitor centre, and a moment later the building burst in a bright orange fireball, and Lex began to cry, and Ellie put her arm around her and tried to get her not to look.

Grant was staring down at the ground, and he had a last glimpse of the hypsilophodonts, leaping gracefully as gazelles, moments before another explosion flared bright beneath them. Their helicopter gained altitude, and then moved east, out over the ocean.

Grant sat back in his seat. He thought of the dinosaurs standing on the beach, and he wondered where they would migrate if they could, and he realised he would never know, and the felt sad and relieved in the same moment.

The officer came forward again, bending close to his face. 'Are you in charge?'

'No,' Grant said.

'Please, señor, who is in charge?'

'Nobody,' Grant said.

The helicopter gained speed as it headed toward the mainland. It was cold now, and the soldiers muscled the door closed. As they did, Grant looked back just once, and saw the island against a deep purple sky and sea, cloaked in a deep mist that blurred the white-hot explosions that burst rapidly, one after another, until it seemed the entire island was glowing, a diminishing bright spot in the darkening night.

Michael Crichton

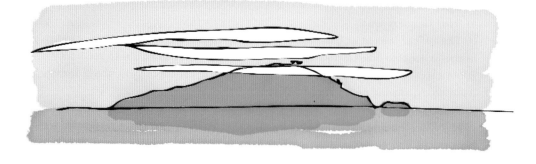

1 Outline, in your own words, what happens in the resolution.
2 What new information do we learn?
3 Is there anything else to discover?
4 Is it a satisfactory ending to the novel? Why or why not?

YOUR TURN

- **Write a list of your three favourite novels and their authors. Put the titles in inverted commas, like this, 'Jurassic Park'.**

- **What type of novels are they – romance, fantasy, realistic, adventure, crime, science fiction or historical?**

- **Write a brief summary of the plot of one of your novels. State where and when it is set. Who are the main characters? What problems do they face?**

- **What do you most like about your favourite novel?**

- **What was the author's purpose in writing the novel – to entertain, to educate, to make you think about something important?**

- **Write the theme in a single sentence, for example, *The theme of this novel is that war is evil.***

DETAILED DESCRIPTIONS

Detailed descriptions help to make a piece of writing more interesting for the reader.

PEOPLE

Here are two descriptive passages. Notice the number of descriptive words used. Descriptive words are called adjectives.

MR WOODFORDE

Mr Woodforde at first glance looked more like an accountant than a physicist. A man of about seventy, he was completely bald and dressed in a neat dark pinstripe suit. He was small and wrinkled and had a mouth full of gold-capped teeth. His skin had the greyish colour of a heavy smoker. His eyes hung like fried eggs, in bags of age.

John Marsden

SHAZ CHRISTIE

Shaz Christie herself was taking the dance class. She was so thin she looked two-dimensional, and so flexible she seemed liquid rather than solid, except that there was a taut, whippy strength about her. She looked like someone from the future, Elaine thought, with her thick black hair that stood straight up from her huge bony forehead and was streaked with glittering silver over each ear. The silver was echoed by a glistening stud in her nose. She was quite tall, as tall as some of the men in the class, and she radiated a kind of ferocious energy that Elaine found both attractive and alarming.

From *Sky Maze* by Gillian Rubenstein

- **Choose two people from the list below and write a detailed description of them. You may like to include details about their hair, eyes, lips, hands, body, legs, voice, clothing and personality.**

PEOPLE

mother
father
girlfriend
boyfriend
sister
brother
bully
doctor
model
aunt
uncle
enemy
dentist

coach
niece
nephew
teacher
grandmother
grandfather
principal
nurse
baby
child
actor
celebrity

Descriptions of places are important as they help you to imagine where the action is happening. In the extract below we see how the author has created a sense of place.

In *The Lord of the Rings*, J.R.R. Tolkien tells how a company of friends and their pony, Bill, set out on an important mission. They travel in distant lands until they come to Moria, built by dwarves. Moria was once beautiful but now it is abandoned and the entrance has been destroyed. Notice how the author creates a sense of dread through his description of the place.

THE LORD OF THE RINGS

The day was drawing to its end, and cold stars were glinting in the sky high above the sunset, when the Company, with all the speed they could, climbed up the slopes and reached the side of the lake. In breadth it looked to be no more than two or three furlongs at the widest point. How far it stretched away southward they could not see in the failing light; but its northern end was no more than half a mile from where they stood, and between the stony ridges that enclosed the valley and the water's edge there was a rim of open ground. They hurried forward, for they had still a mile or two to go before they could reach the point on the far shore that Gandalf was making for and then he had still to find the doors.

When they came to the northernmost corner of the lake they found a narrow creek that barred their way. It was green and stagnant, thrust out like a slimy arm towards the enclosing hills. Gimli strode forward undeterred, and found that the water was shallow, no more than ankle deep at the edge. Behind him they walked in file, threading their way with care, for under the weedy pools were sliding and greasy stones, and footing was treacherous. Frodo shuddered with disgust at the touch of the dark unclean water on his feet.

As Sam, the last of the Company, led Bill up on to the dry ground on the far side, there came a soft sound: a swish, followed by a plop, as if a fish had disturbed the still surface of the water. Turning quickly they saw ripples, black-edged with shadow in the waning light: great rings were widening outwards from a point far out in the lake. There was a bubbling noise, and then silence. The dusk deepened, and the last gleams of the sunset were veiled in cloud.

Gandalf now pressed on at a great pace, and the others followed as quickly as they could. They reached the strip of dry land between the lake and the cliffs: it was narrow, often hardly a dozen yards across, and encumbered with fallen rock and stones; but they found a way, hugging the cliff, and keeping as far from the dark water as they might. A mile southwards along the shore they came upon holly trees. Stumps and dead boughs were rotting in the

shallows, the remains it seemed of old thickets, or of a hedge that had once lined the road across the drowned valley. But close under the cliff there stood, still strong and living, two tall trees, larger than any trees of holly that Frodo had ever seen or imagined. Their great roots spread from the wall to the water. Under the looming cliffs they had looked like mere bushes, when seen far off from the top of the Stair; but now they towered overhead, stiff, dark, and silent, throwing deep night-shadows about their feet, standing like sentinel pillars at the end of the road.

J.R.R. Tolkien

YOUR TURN

The setting of a story is the time and place where the action occurs. It is very important.

- **Choose two of the settings below and describe them in detail:**

  - **classroom**
  - **supermarket**
  - **volcano**
  - **stadium**
  - **attic**

  - **kitchen**
  - **haunted house**
  - **restaurant**
  - **garage**

  - **beach**
  - **hospital**
  - **park**
  - **library**

WEATHER

Descriptions of seasons and the weather often can create a mood or atmosphere. Here are two contrasting descriptions of the seaside at different times of the year.

WINTER

Winter will bring cold, starry nights and damp morning mists that rise from the lake in a white cloud. Strong winds will start up along the seafront, rolling balls of yellow foam along the beach, and the sand will be wet and hard from the driving rain. Seagulls will be standing in the wind like old men at bus stops, and the pelicans on the mooring buoys will huddle together, jamming their bills behind their wing feathers. You won't see a single boat on the lake, they'll all be tied up at the boatsheds, their motors covered with canvas hoods. Nobody will be on the main street. It'll be like High Noon, with the gunslingers waiting for Gary Cooper to ride in.

From Boys by the Sea by Barry Donnelly

THE BEACH

August Bank Holiday. A tune on an ice-cream cornet. A slap of sea and a tickle of sand. A fanfare of sunshades opening. A wince and whinny of bathers dancing into deceptive water. A tuck of dresses. A rolling of trousers. A compromise of paddlers. A sunburn of girls and a lark of boys.

A silent hullabaloo of balloons.

Children all day capered or squealed by the glazed or bashing sea, and the steam-organ wheezed its waltzes in the threadbare playground and the waste lot, where the dodgems dodged, behind the pickle factory.

From *Holiday Memory* by Dylan Thomas

YOUR TURN

- Describe two of the following scenes. Try to describe the sights, sounds, and smells of each:
  - a heat wave in the city
  - a cool evening
  - a windy night
  - a thunderstorm
  - a grand prix (Formula One)
  - a frosty morning in the countryside
  - a motorcycle race

FRONT AND BACK COVERS

The covers of novels are designed to attract readers. The title, author and publisher's name appear on the front cover. A summary of the story is usually given on the back.

Look at and read the front and back covers below and answer the questions that follow.

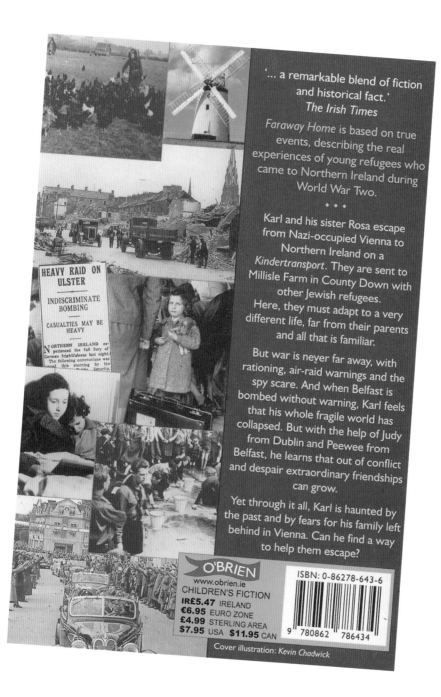

You can see the latest cover deisgn for *Faraway Home* by Marilyn Taylor, published by The O'Brien Press Ltd, at www.obrien.ie

1   What is the title of this novel?

2   Give the name of the author and the publisher.

3   What indications are there on the front cover that the story is set in Ireland?

4   Comment on the use of colour in the illustration on the front cover.

5   Read the summary of the story, on the back cover. Who are the main characters?

6   What do you think the word 'kindertransport' means?

7   Why does the summary end with a question?

8   Study the photographs on the back cover carefully. Which ones were taken in Vienna? Which ones were taken in Ireland?

9   Can you trace the plot through the photographs? Explain your answer.

10   Comment on the use of colour in the different photographs.

11   Why did the publisher decide to use a drawing on the front cover and photographs on the back?

12   Would these covers entice you to read this novel? Give reasons for your answer.

YOUR TURN

- **Design a cover for your favourite novel.**

- **Write a brief summary of the story for the back cover in order to persuade someone to buy the book. Do not reveal the ending. You may model your summary on the one shown here.**

- **Analyse the cover of the novel you are now reading. Comment on and try to account for:**

  – the style and the size of the lettering

  – the illustration (if any)

  – the use of colour

  – the position of the title and the author's name

  – any other material that is printed on the cover

CHAPTER 5

NOUNS AND PRONOUNS

WHAT YOU WILL LEARN IN THIS CHAPTER

- **The different types of nouns – common, proper, abstract and collective**
- **How the form of pronouns changes as you use them in different ways in your speech and writing**

HOW YOU WILL LEARN

- **Identifying nouns and pronouns in different contexts**
- **Matching nouns with their meanings**
- **Writing different exercises which focus on types of nouns and the pictures they create in the minds of readers**

INTRODUCING NOUNS

Words are everywhere – we speak, read, hear and write words. Words continually attract and fascinate us because they add so much meaning to the way we relate to others.

Nouns are the naming words in our language – they name the people, objects and animals we meet in our daily lives. They also name feelings such as love and hate and qualities such as beauty and intelligence. There are also nouns for collections of people, animals and things.

The four kinds of nouns are:
- **Common**
- **Proper**
- **Abstract**
- **Collective**

Ready . . .
I will be the **winner** –
I possess the **skill**,
the **knowledge** and
the **will**.

Set . . .
Are my **runners** properly
set on the **blocks**?
Are my **hands** in their correct
positions?

GO!
I have a great **feeling**
of **excitement** but I
must control my **speed**!
I must get past the **crowd**
but I must also reserve **power**
for the **sprint** at the **finish**!

COMMON NOUNS

Common nouns are words used to name any person, animal, place or thing. Common nouns are found everywhere.

Here is a street scene full of common nouns:

fence	exhaust
trees	mirror
parrot	curtains
hair	fish
car	dog
helmet	man
woman	cat
shop	sunglasses
umbrella	teeth
pram	tyres

YOUR TURN

SHOPPING FOR COMMON NOUNS

Look at the supermarket scene and identify and write down ten common nouns in the picture.

PROPER NOUNS

Proper nouns are easily identified because they always start with a capital letter. A proper noun is the name of a particular person, place or thing.

Here is a special place, a special person and a special object. Each name is a proper noun.

Uluru

Nelson Mandela

The Eiffel Tower

NOUNS AND THEIR MEANINGS

For each of the meanings below, supply a common or a proper noun from the list.

library	telescope	shirt	potato	dentist
Mars	Shakespeare	cup	Joan of Arc	Buddha
dictionary	Malaysia	clock	Mozart	teacher
Everest	hat	Volvo	ladder	Pacific
astronaut	Bono	Einstein	Tokyo	Vesuvius
Madonna	zoo	toe	dog	California

Meanings

1 An animal that barks.
2 A container to drink from.
3 The founder of a great religion.
4 One of the ten parts that end the foot.
5 The capital city of Japan.
6 A garment for the upper body.
7 A planet in the solar system.
8 An Irish celebrity.
9 One who instructs.
10 A basic food that grows underground.
11 An Asian country.
12 A device for climbing up and down.
13 The great English playwright.
14 A device that shows you the time.
15 A protection for the head.
16 The world's highest mountain.
17 A French heroine.
18 The world's biggest ocean.
19 A place where animals are kept.
20 A device that enlarges images.
21 A book of words and their meanings.
22 The make of a famous car.
23 A person who travels in space.
24 The 'Film Star State'.

25 A place where books are kept.

26 A person who cares for the teeth.

27 A famous volcano.

28 A famous composer.

29 A famous scientist.

30 A famous pop star.

COLLECTIVE NOUNS

A collective noun is a word used for a collection or group of persons, animals or things, for example, herd and gang.

The passage below uses various collective nouns.

As far as the eye could see across the vast African plain, herds of wild animals grazed. The closest was a herd of zebras. It was a beautiful natural sight. However, among the long grass nearby, other eyes were watching. A pride of lions, their tails lashing from side to side, gazed hungrily at the zebras. Hidden somewhere nearby was the pack of hyenas that always follows a pride of lions, awaiting their turn to steal the remains of the kill after the lions had gorged themselves. Our group of tourists was glad of the vehicle's protection.

Insert the correct collective noun from the list below for each of the phrases.

litter   galaxy   swarm   crowd
bunch   flock   army   hand
batch   choir   roll   school
flight   fleet   pod   cluster
bouquet   pack   band   peal
board   album   library   plague

 1 a . . . . of locusts
 2 a . . . . of cards
 3 a . . . . of kittens
 4 a . . . . of flowers
 5 a . . . . of grapes
 6 an . . . . . . of photos
 7 a . . . . of books
 8 a . . . . of whales
 9 an . . . . . . of soldiers
10 a . . . . of fish
11 a . . . . of planes
12 a . . . . of musicians
13 a . . . . of bells
14 a . . . . of diamonds
15 a . . . . of singers
16 a . . . . of banknotes
17 a . . . . of bees
18 a . . . . of stars
19 a . . . . of spectators
20 a . . . . of birds
21 a . . . . of scones
22 a . . . . of directors
23 a . . . . of ships
24 a . . . . of bananas

ABSTRACT NOUNS

The word 'abstract' refers to things that have no real or physical existence. Abstract nouns are words that name qualities, emotions and actions, for example, excitement, truth, love, anger, joy and peace. They are usually things you cannot see or touch.

The cheetah is a noble animal whose nature can be described in terms of abstract nouns.

courage	freedom
power	ferocity
strength	cunning
speed	stealth
beauty	patience

CHOOSING ABSTRACT NOUNS

Choose the abstract noun from each of the following groups of words.

1	animal	cat	Felix	luck
2	person	selfishness	coat	Rosemary
3	stamina	swim	speed	waves
4	bird	flock	flight	wing
5	painting	draw	beauty	sculpture
6	dog	loyalty	bone	barking
7	car	road	fear	accident
8	doctor	nurse	skill	disease
9	soldier	war	Germany	horror
10	astronaut	power	moon	Venus
11	dentist	tooth	pain	drill
12	church	St Peters	priest	faith
13	body	head	wisdom	brain

14	house	food	shelter	life
15	effort	sport	champion	winner
16	library	book	knowledge	catalogue
17	painting	artist	palette	inspiration
18	bank	money	prosperity	coins
19	school	learning	teacher	student
20	radio	television	newspaper	persuasion

ABSTRACT NOUNS IN PROVERBS AND SAYINGS

The abstract nouns have been removed from these well-known proverbs and sayings. Choose the abstract nouns from the list below and complete the proverbs and sayings. First letters are given to help you.

1. B . . . . is only skin deep.
2. A little k . . . . is a dangerous thing.
3. L . . . . will find a way.
4. C . . . . does not pay.
5. N . . . . is the mother of invention.
6. T . . . . is stranger than fiction.
7. F . . . . favours the brave.
8. T . . . . is a great healer.
9. H . . . . is the best policy.
10. A . . . . makes the heart grow fonder.
11. R . . . . is sweet.
12. There is s . . . . in numbers.
13. S . . . . is golden.
14. Empty vessels make the most n . . . .
15. C . . . . begins at home.
16. The more h . . . . the less s . . . . .

honesty	beauty	love	knowledge	
revenge	safety	silence	fortune	charity
absence	haste	truth	necessity	
noise	speed	time	crime	

NOUNS PUT PEOPLE IN THEIR PLACE

Match up the people in the left column with the places they would be found from the right column.

People

cook
nurse
swimmer
sailor
teacher
pilot
judge
skater
gambler
climber
teller
driver
mechanic
toddler
queen
actor
jockey
politician
priest
soldier

Places

barracks
workshop
ship
bus
kindergarten
church
parliament
racecourse
hospital
plane
school
palace
stage
court
kitchen
rink
mountain
pool
casino
bank

NOUNS IN LIMERICKS

The rhyming nouns that complete the following limerick have been removed and placed in the panel. Fit the rhyming words back into their limerick.

THE YOUNG MAN FROM BENGAL

There was a young man from ....
Who went to a fancy-dress ....
He went just for ....
Dressed up as a ....
And a dog ate him up in the ....

| bun | Bengal | hall | fun | ball |

YOUR TURN

Create your own sporting poster on one of the following sports using twenty nouns to describe a picture.

Topics

Tennis

Golf

Swimming

Scuba diving

Football

Skiing

Cricket

Volleyball

Basketball

Sailing

Canoeing

Horse riding

Abseiling

Fishing

Cycling

Orienteering

Hurling

PRONOUNS

Pronouns may be used instead of nouns. A personal pronoun takes the place of a person's name.

Here is a table of personal pronouns.

First person singular	I	me	myself
Second person singular	You	you	yourself
Third person singular	He	him	himself
Third person singular	She	her	herself
Third person singular	It	it	itself
First person plural	We	us	ourselves
Second person plural	You	you	yourselves
Third person plural	They	them	themselves

Possessive pronouns indicate ownership. Here is a list of possessive pronouns.

Mine	Its
Yours	Ours
His	Yours
Hers	Theirs

Relative pronouns refer to the noun in the sentence.

Who, whose, which and that are relative pronouns.

WHO refers to people only.

The student who came first in the summer examinations studied every day.

WHOSE indicates ownership.

That's the man whose car was stolen.

WHICH refers to things only.

Which book is more interesting?

THAT can refer to people and things.

There is the book that he lost.
There is the mountaineer that climbed Mt Everest.

PRONOUNS IN ACTION

FIRST PERSON

Here is an example of the use of first person pronouns in a diary entry from *The Secret Diary of Adrian Mole aged 13³/₄* by Sue Townsend. Read the entry and write down all the first person pronouns you can find.

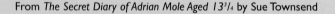

THURSDAY FEBRUARY 12TH

I found my mother dyeing her hair in the bathroom tonight. This has come as a complete shock to me. For thirteen and three-quarter years I have thought I had a mother with red hair, now I find out that it is really light brown. My mother asked me not to tell my father. What a state their marriage must be in.

From *The Secret Diary of Adrian Mole Aged 13³/₄* by Sue Townsend

SECOND PERSON

Read the passage below and jot down the second person pronouns that you find.

HOLIDAY OF A LIFETIME

Do you want to have a holiday of a lifetime, where you can swim to your heart's content on beautiful white sandy beaches? Perhaps you enjoy pleasant strolls through beautiful bush land. You won't want to miss the amazing natural wonders of our sanctuaries and wildlife parks.
Everything is here for you and your family at Paradise Resort on the Sunshine Coast. All you need to do is ring your travel agent now.

THIRD PERSON

Writers often use the third person because they can describe the thoughts, emotions and actions of all the characters in the text. Most short stories and novels are written in the third person.

Read this description from the novel *The Demon Headmaster* by Gillian Cross. Write down the third person pronouns in the passage.

THE DEMON HEADMASTER

A s she stepped through, Dinah glanced quickly round the room. It was the tidiest office she had ever seen. There were no papers, no files, no pictures on the walls. Just a large empty-topped desk, a filing cabinet and a bookcase with a neat row of books.

She took it all in in one second and then forgot it as her eyes fell on the man standing by the window. He was tall and thin, dressed in an immaculate black suit. From his shoulders, a long, black teacher's gown hung in heavy folds, like wings, giving him the appearance of a huge crow. Only his head was startlingly white. Fair hair, almost as colourless as snow, lay round a face with paper-white skin and pallid lips. His eyes were hidden behind dark glasses, like two black holes in the middle of whiteness.

From *The Demon Headmaster* by Gillian Cross

YOUR TURN

PRONOUNS IN COMIC STRIPS

Writers are always using pronouns and cartoonists are no exception. Write down next to each comic strip the pronouns that the cartoonists have used.

CHAPTER 6

LETTER WRITING

WHAT YOU WILL LEARN IN THIS CHAPTER

- How to recognise different types of letters
- How to structure a personal letter and a formal letter

HOW YOU WILL LEARN

- Reading samples of letters
- Writing your own letters

INTRODUCING LETTERS

Letters are an important means of communication. We can write letters to express our emotions or our opinions, to inform or seek information, to keep in touch with our family and friends, to complain, to apply for work, to send or accept an invitation, and to say thank you. Letters may be personal or formal.

PERSONAL LETTERS

These letters, taken from the introduction to *Where Rainbows End* by Cecelia Ahern, are examples of personal letters.

To Alex
  You are invited to my 7th birthday party on Tuesday the 8th of April in my house. We are having a magician and you can come to my house at 2 o'clock. It is over at 5 o'clock. I hope you will come.
  From your best friend Rosie

To Rosie
  Yes I will come to your brithday party on Wensday.
  Form Alex

To Alex

My birthday party is on Tuesday not Wednesday. You can't bring sandy to the party because mum says so. She is a smelly dog.

From Rosie

To Rosie

I do not care wot your stupid mum says sandy wants to come.

Form Alex

To Alex

My mum is not stupid you are. You are not aloud to bring the dog. She will brust the balloons.

From Rosie

To Rosie

Then I am not going.

From Alex

To Alex

Fine.

From Rosie

Dear Mrs Stewart,

I just called to have a word with you about my daughter Rosie's birthday on the 8th of April. Sorry you weren't in, but I'll drop by again later this afternoon and maybe we can talk then.

There seems to be some sort of little problem with Alex and Rosie lately. I think they're not quite on talking terms. I hope you can fill me in on the situation when we meet. Rosie would really love if he came to her birthday party.

I'm looking forward to meeting the mother of this charming young man!

See you then,

Alice Dunne

To Rosie

I would be happy to go to your brithday party next week. Thank you fro inviting me and sandy.

From Alex your frend

1 Give the full names of the characters who write letters in this extract.

2 How old are the children? When is Rosie's birthday?

3 What do we learn about Alex from reading his letters?

4 What is your impression of Rosie's mother? Refer to the text in your answer.

5 What do you think happened when the mothers met? Are there any clues in Alex's letter?

FEATURES OF PERSONAL LETTERS

While these letters are acceptable because they are written by young children, hopefully the standard of your personal letters will be much higher!

Here are the features and the layout of personal letters to help you improve your writing.

Greeting   The opening is casual and friendly.

Content   The body of the letter is concerned with news about yourself, your family, and your friends.

It is written in paragraphs. Each paragraph should deal with one main topic, such as your holiday, activities in your school etc.

If possible, refer to something that happened the last time you met or heard from your friend or relative. You can ask questions or make comments if you wish.

Remember to make it as interesting as you can. It should be the type of letter you would like to receive!

Tone   Personal letters are friendly, conversational and relaxed in style and tone.

Ending   The ending is friendly and informal.

Signature   Sign your first name clearly at the end of the letter.

Your Address _____

_____

_____

_____

Date _____

STRUCTURE OF PERSONAL LETTERS

Dear _____ ,

Paragraph One _____

_____

_____

_____

_____

_____

Paragraph Two _____

_____

_____

_____

_____

Paragraph Three _____

_____

_____

_____

_____

_____

Best wishes,
Signature _____

These personal letters will help you to write your own letters later.

10 Main St.,
Newtown,
Co. Leitrim — Home address

1st July, 20___ — Date

Greeting — **Dear Ann,**

I was delighted to receive your postcard from Spain. Your resort looked absolutely gorgeous. I am really impatient to hear all about the wonderful time you had on the Costa Brava. Unfortunately we are not going on holidays this year. Dad said the cost of the extension to the house means it will be at least ten years before we go away again, but he was only joking . . . I think!

That's the bad news. Now comes the good part. Mum said that as we are not going away this summer and the new spare bedroom is free, you might like to visit us for three weeks, when you have recovered from the jet-lag. We could laze around, go horse-riding, have picnics by the river and go to the local disco on Friday night. My big brother has actually volunteered to drive us home. I think he still has a major crush on you – he never drives me anywhere, except up the walls!

Let me know as soon as possible if you can come, so that we can make plans.

Best wishes, — Friendly closure

Mary — Signature

10 Main St.,
Newtown,
Co. Leitrim

8th July, 20___

Hi Jean-Luc,

Thanks for your last letter. Glad to hear that your exams went well. I finished school over four weeks ago and began work in our local garage on a part-time basis. The extension to the house is finished also, so life is getting back to normal here . . . almost.

The bad news is that my younger sister invited her geeky friend, Ann, to stay for three weeks and the little horror accepted. Mary has convinced Ann that I am madly in love with her and the thought of a moony-eyed fifteen year old following me around for the rest of the month makes me sick. However there are some advantages. Dad bribed me to 'volunteer' to drive them home from the local disco. Better still, my parents have agreed to let me visit you in August, on condition that I 'behave myself' while the little pest is here.

My mother will ring yours to work out the details. Your invitation to spend the holidays with you in France could not have come at a better time!

Hope to see you soon,
Michael

FORMAL LETTERS

Formal letters are very different in tone and content from personal letters. They are businesslike, get to the point quickly and are never gossipy, personal or amusing. They are written when you wish to apply for a job, seek and send information, or make a complaint.

FEATURES OF FORMAL LETTERS

Greeting
The greeting is always formal.

If you know the name of the person to whom you are writing begin with 'Dear Mr/Ms/Dr' etc.

If you do not know the name write 'Dear Sir/Madam'.

Content
Keep the letter short and to the point. Do not include any unnecessary information. The content should be factual and written in a logical manner. It is therefore a good idea to plan your letter before you start to write.

Tone
The tone of formal letters is businesslike, formal and polite.

Ending
End with 'Yours sincerely' if you know the name of the person receiving the letter.

End with 'Yours faithfully' if the letter begins 'Dear Sir/Madam', 'Dear Parent/Guardian' etc.

Signature
Always end with your full signature.

STRUCTURE OF FORMAL LETTERS

Your Address ____________________

____

____

____

Date ____________________

Name (if known) ____________________

Title ____________________

Address ____________________

____

____

____

Dear ____________________ ,

Paragraph One ____________________

____

____

____

Paragraph Two ____________________

____

____

____

Paragraph Three ____________________

____

____

____

Yours faithfully/sincerely,

John Brown

Formal letters look like the following examples.

10 Main St.,
Newtown,
Co. Leitrim — Home address

1st June, 20___ — Date

Name — **Mr John Lynch,**

Title — **The Manager,**

Business address —
Pitstop Garage,
High St.,
Newtown,
Co. Leitrim

Formal greeting — **Dear Mr Lynch,**

    I wish to apply for the position of garage attendant as advertised in 'The Leitrim Press', on Monday, 30th May.

    At present I am a Third Year student in Newtown Secondary School, studying for my Junior Certificate examination. I will be available for work from the 15th June. My previous work experience includes working in a garage in Oldford, last summer.

    I have enclosed a copy of my Curriculum Vitae with the names of three referees, as requested.

Formal closure — **Yours sincerely,**

Chris O'Neill

Here is Chris O'Neill's Curriculum Vitae. Fill in the blanks for him. Some of the information can be found in his letter. You will have to use your imagination also!

CURRICULUM VITAE

Name Chris O'Neill

Address   Telephone No. 123 45 67

Date of Birth

Schools Attended

Work Experience

Interests/Hobbies

Referees

Mr Brian Garvey,	Mr Patrick Murphy,	Ms Deirdre O'Shea,
Oldford Garage,	Principal,	Castleview Road,
Oldford,	Newtown Secondary	Newtown,
Co. Leitrim	School,	Co. Leitrim
	Newtown,	
	Co. Leitrim	

Write out your own Curriculum Vitae using the headings in the example.

10 Main St.,
Newtown,
Co. Leitrim

1st June, 20____

The Manager,
'Ready To Wear',
Side Row,
Newtown,
Co. Leitrim

Dear Sir/Madam,

On Saturday, 30th May, I purchased a leather jacket at a sale in your shop. When I took the jacket home I discovered the zip did not work properly.

I returned immediately to your shop with the receipt, but the assistant refused to exchange it for another jacket. She claimed it was in perfect condition when it was sold and suggested I damaged the zip when fitting it on at home. Even a quick examination will prove that the zip was sewn on incorrectly.

I insist on my rights as a consumer to an exchange or a full refund. Please contact me at the above address as soon as possible so that this matter can be resolved quickly.

Yours faithfully,

_____

T.J. O'Neill

10 Main St.,
Newtown,
Co. Leitrim

Home address

21st Sept, 20_____

Date

Name
Ms Jane Lynch,

Title
Information Officer,

Businesss address
HITEK,
Newtown Industrial Estate,
Newtown,
Co. Leitrim

Formal greeting
Dear Ms Lynch,

    I am a Transition Year student in Newtown School. As part of our course this year, we are required to do a project on a major industry in our area. I hope you can help. I need information on

- the number of people you employ
- the type of goods you produce
- the source of your raw materials
- your markets.

I would be very grateful for any help you can give me.

Formal closure
Yours sincerely,

_____

Chris O'Neill

- **Write a letter to:**
- **your pen pal, inviting him or her to stay with you for two weeks during the holidays**
- **your aunt, thanking her for a gift she sent you**
- **the manager of a restaurant, complaining about a meal you had there**
- **a famous person, inviting him or her to open the new extension to your school**
- **the information officer in an embassy, requesting information for a geography project**
- **a local shop, hotel, garage or company, applying for a summer job**

In the novel *Harry Potter and the Prisoner of Azkaban,* by J.K. Rowling, the young wizard is spending his holidays with his relatives at number four Privet Drive. On his birthday, his owl arrives with a letter and gift from Hermione. She writes about Ron Weasley who is in their class at Hogwarts, where Ron's brother has become head boy. A second owl has brought a letter from Hogwarts.

Dear Harry,

Ron wrote to me and told me about his phone call to your Uncle Vernon, I do hope you're all right.

I'm on holiday in France at the moment, and I didn't know how I was going to send this to you – what if they'd opened it at Customs? – but then Hedwig turned up! I think she wanted to make sure you got something for your birthday for a change. I bought your present by owl-order; there was an advertisement in the Daily Prophet (I've been getting it delivered, it's so good to keep up with what's going on in the wizarding world). Did you see that picture of Ron and his family a week ago? I bet he's learning loads, I'm really jealous – the ancient Egyptian wizards are fascinating.

There's some interesting local history of witchcraft here, too. I've re-written my whole History of Magic essay to include some of the things I've found out. I hope it's not too long, it's two rolls of parchment more than Professor Binns asked for.

Ron says he's going to be in London in the last week of the holidays. Can you make it? Will your aunt and uncle let you come? I really hope you can. If not, I'll see you on the Hogwarts Express on September the first!

Love from

Hermione

P.S. Ron says Percy's Head Boy. I'll bet Percy's really pleased. Ron doesn't seem too happy about it.

Dear Mr Potter,

Please note that the new school year will begin on September the first. The Hogwarts Express will leave from King's Cross Station, platform nine and three-quarters, at eleven o'clock.

Third-years are permitted to visit the village of Hogsmeade at certain weekends. Please give the enclosed permission form to your parent or guardian to sign.

A list of books for next year is enclosed.

Yours sincerely,

Professor M. McGonagall

Deputy Headmistress

 **EXPLORING THE TEXT**

1 Where is Ron spending his holidays?

2 When does the new school year begin?

3 What privileges are given to Third Years?

4 What do we learn about Hermione, based on her letter only?

5 Which of these letters is personal and which is formal? How do you know? Refer to the texts in your answer.

YOUR TURN

- **Write out the following addresses correctly:**

- **your own address**

- **your best friend's address**

- **an imaginary address**

- **Write out today's date.**

- **Here are some typical closures: 'Yours faithfully', 'Best wishes', 'Yours sincerely', 'Love', 'Take care'. Match them to the greetings below.**

Dear Mam

Hi John

Dear Mr Smythe

Hello Ann

Dear Sir

Dear Pierre

Sir/Madam

- **Write to your favourite author explaining why you like his or her novels. You may like to state:**
  - **when you started to read the novels**
  - **how you first came across them – in a library, a bookshop, as a present, they were recommended by a friend**
  - **your favourite book by the author**
  - **what you most like about it and what you least like**
  - **any other information or comments that you think are relevant**

Hint

Before you begin writing, decide if this is a personal or a formal letter and then follow the correct layout. Remember to include the date and your signature!

CHAPTER 7

VERBS

WHAT YOU WILL LEARN IN THIS CHAPTER

- How verbs express actions, feelings and thoughts
- The effect of verbs in different types of texts
- How verbs express time

HOW YOU WILL LEARN

- Identifying verbs in different contexts
- Exploring the use of verbs in texts

INTRODUCING VERBS

Verbs express all kinds of actions. They are words that communicate actions such as doing, being, having, talking, feeling and thinking.

A verb can be one word, for example, 'The monster **lifted** its head'. But quite often it will be made up of several words, for example, 'Its giant feet **were thundering** on the ground'.

> Words that help to complete the verbs are called auxiliary verbs. The main auxiliary verbs are: am, is, are, be, was, were, shall, will, should, could, would, has, have, had, may, might, do, did, can.

The dinosaur **has escaped** from Jurassic Park!

Its fierce eyes **had spied** the visitors.

The park visitors **were screaming** at the beast.

It **will attack** without warning.

Its massive tail **was shaking** the ground.

It **is roaring** loudly.

The visitors **will survive** if they can outrun the beast.

Their movements **had angered** the monster.

They **were shouting** encouragement to each other.

VERBS AND TEXTS

Verbs appear everywhere – in poems, novels, plays and most other texts. The novel extract below from *The Lost World* by Sir Arthur Conan Doyle is full of action verbs.

ENCOUNTER WITH A DINOSAUR

I **stood** paralysed on the path. Then suddenly I **saw** it. A great, dark shadow **came** out of the bushes and **hopped** into the moonlight. The beast **moved** like a kangaroo. It **was springing** along on its powerful hindlegs while its front ones **were held** bent in front of it. It **was** of enormous size and power, like an elephant standing upright. This beast **had** a squat, toad-like face. It **was** surely one of the great flesh-eating dinosaurs, the most terrible beasts that **have** ever **walked** this earth.

As the huge beast **loped** along, it **dropped** forward upon its forepaws and **brought** its nose to the ground every so often. It **was smelling** out my trail. Soon it **came bounding** swiftly along the path I **had taken**.

From *The Lost World* by Sir Arthur Conan Doyle

FIND THE VERBS

Pick out the verbs in the following scene from *The Lost World*.

CHASED BY A DINOSAUR

I **fled**! Up to then the dinosaur had hunted by scent and his movement was slow. But he had seen me as I ran. Now he hunted by sight for the path showed him where I had gone. As he came round the curve he was springing in great bounds. The moonlight shone upon his huge projecting eyes, the row of enormous teeth in his open mouth and the gleaming fringe of claws growing out of his short, powerful forearms. I screamed with terror, turned and rushed wildly down the path. Behind me, the thick gasps of his breathing sounded louder and louder. Every instant, I expected to feel his grip upon my back. And then, suddenly, there came a crash – I was falling through space and everything beyond was darkness and rest.

From *The Lost World* by Sir Arthur Conan Doyle

EVERYDAY VERBS THAT COMMAND

Complete each of the following expressions with everyday verbs that command.

1   L . . . . to the radio.

2   W . . . . television.

3   W . . . . the flag.

4   B . . . . a ticket.

5   W . . . . your hands.

6   S . . . . a song.

7   S . . . . a boat.

8   H . . . . a nail.

9   P . . . . a drink.

10   W . . . . a letter.

VERBS TELL WHEN

Verbs tell us when an action is taking place.

	Present	Past	Future
First person	I am	was	will
Second person	You are	were	will
Third person	He/She/It is	was	will
First person plural	We are	were	will
Second person plural	You are	were	will
Third person plural	They are	were	will

PRESENT AND PAST

Below are two columns of verbs in present and past tense. Insert in the spaces the verb forms that are missing. The first has been done to help you.

	Present	Past		Present	Past
1	She knows	She knew	**13**	We drive	. . . .
2	. . . .	It fell	**14**	. . . .	They saw
3	She leaves	. . . .	**15**	We do	. . . .
4	. . . .	I began	**16**	. . . .	It crept
5	He drinks	. . . .	**17**	They are	. . . .
6	. . . .	It hid	**18**	. . . .	She sang
7	We meet	. . . .	**19**	We bring	. . . .
8	. . . .	You went	**20**	. . . .	He wrote
9	They fight	. . . .	**21**	She gives	. . . .
10	. . . .	I ate	**22**	. . . .	It grew
11	He stands	. . . .	**23**	They buy	. . . .
12	. . . .	She caught	**24**	. . . .	I drove

The Diary of Adrian Mole is a novel made up of diary entries written by a young boy named Adrian. Here is a page from his diary listing his New Year's resolutions.

FUTURE TENSE

Thursday January 1st

These are my New Year's resolutions:
1 I will help the blind across the road.
2 I will hang my trousers up.
3 I will put the sleeves back on my records.
4 I will not start smoking.
5 I will stop squeezing my spots.
6 I will be kind to the dog.
7 I will help the poor and ignorant.
8 After hearing the disgusting noises from downstairs last night, I have also vowed never to drink alcohol.

EXPRESSIVE VERBS

Verbs such as said and want are frequently over-used. Write out the following dialogue, replacing each said with a more expressive verb from inside the football.

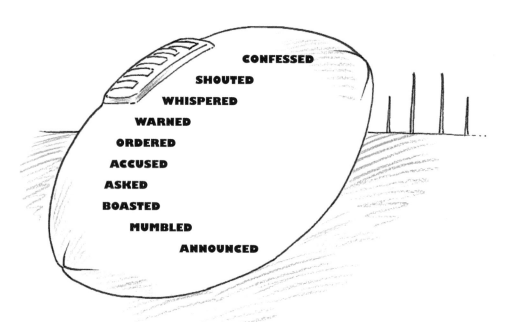

CONFESSED
SHOUTED
WHISPERED
WARNED
ORDERED
ACCUSED
ASKED
BOASTED
MUMBLED
ANNOUNCED

'Our next footy practice will be held on Tuesday,' said the coach. 'And,' he said 'if we don't perform better at the next game, we will be eliminated from the finals.'

'Any questions?' said the coach.

'I had the highest score last time,' said one player.

'Yes, and you even scored against your own team,' said another player.

'BE QUIET!' said the coach.

'Coach, it was my fault we didn't win,' said a third player.

A player chewing gum said indistinctly, 'Don't blame me.'

'Wait until you've finished chewing before you speak,' said the coach.

'I don't like football,' said a player in a low voice.

CHAPTER 8

FACTUAL TEXTS

WHAT YOU WILL LEARN IN THIS CHAPTER

- How to plan your writing
- The purpose and register of your writing
- The effects of your writing on the audience
- How to draft a text
- The way reports, diaries, reviews, instructions and explanations are constructed

HOW YOU WILL LEARN

- Examining the effects of audience, purpose, register and text types on your writing
- Writing your own version of factual texts
- Exploring the way meaning is conveyed in a range of texts
- Modelling your writing on sample texts

INTRODUCING FACTUAL TEXTS

We live in the information age, surrounded by factual texts. Information is available at our fingertips through the Internet and computers, and through printed sources such as books, newspapers, magazines and posters. Factual texts refer to informative texts. This includes instructions, reports, explanations, descriptions and reviews. In the following pages you will learn how to plan and write your own factual texts.

STARTING OFF

●●●●●●

Before you begin writing factual texts you should make out a plan. A good plan helps you to communicate your ideas clearly and effectively. When planning your work you should consider the title, the purpose of the text, its layout, your audience and the type of language you will use.

TITLE

Write down the title of your work so that you can focus on the topic you intend to tackle. Refer back to the title every so often so that you do not wander off the point.

PURPOSE

Know why you are writing the text. Do you want to inform, instruct, explain, describe, review or relate something? The purpose of the text may affect its shape or structure.

STRUCTURE

A speech, report, explanation and recipe have different structures. It is important to know their shapes.

AUDIENCE

The people listening to or reading your text are known as your audience. Your audience may be mainly young children, teenagers, adults, community leaders, students, parents, teachers or the general public. The words you use should take into account their age, background and needs.

REGISTER

You must choose your words to suit your audience, if you wish to communicate your message successfully. For example, you would not use the same language when speaking to a group of very young children and a group of university lecturers. If your audience does not understand the words you use you have failed to deliver your message. You must suit your language to your audience.

WRITING A DRAFT

Writing is an essential means of communication in everyday life. You will often need to write letters, notes, messages and probably reports and reviews of all kinds. Writing is also a way of sharing your feelings and the power of your imagination with others.

You can practise preparing to write by choosing a topic then jotting down all the ideas that come into your mind as freely and rapidly as you can. As one idea leads to another, you will soon find that you have a rough plan on which a story can be based.

Suppose you are given skateboarding as a topic to write about, your ideas might look like this:

JOTTING DOWN YOUR IDEAS

- Skateboarding in my life
- My best memory of skateboarding
- My most exciting skateboarding experience
- The dangers of skateboarding
- Going for the big jump
- What skateboarding means to me

After you have jotted down your ideas, the next step is to organise them in the way you think will be interesting and effective for a reader. Your writing plan might finally be set out in this pattern:

ORGANISING YOUR IDEAS

- ✔ Skateboarding in my life
- ✔ What skateboarding means to me
- ✔ The dangers of skateboarding
- ✔ My most exciting skateboarding experience
- ✔ Going for the big jump
- ✔ My best memory of skateboarding

As you prepare your writing plan, you need to consider the interests and outlook of the reader. Often a consideration of the reader guides you in your choice of the ideas you select.

YOUR FIRST DRAFT

Almost all writers find that they need to revise or rewrite their original thoughts in order to communicate exactly what they want to say. The series of steps a writer uses in revising and rewriting is called writing a draft. Writing a draft involves rearranging, changing, adding and deleting words until finally the writer is satisfied.

Your first draft is your first attempt to expand the ideas you have jotted down for your piece of writing. It is important to think of your first draft as a piece of writing that needs to be improved in various ways. The changes may involve your choice of words, spelling, the placement of phrases and the rearrangement of sentences and paragraphs to make your ideas flow freely and clearly.

Here are the ideas on the topic of skateboarding expanded into a first draft. Notice how the writer has worked on this first draft to improve it.

SKATEBOARDING IN MY LIFE

Skateboard*ing* is very important in my life because it is *an* enjoyable way to fill ~~your~~ *my* leisure time. I de*c*ided it would also give me plenty of sunshine, ~~and~~ fresh air and exercise*s*.

However, you need to be *an* experienced skateboarder to realise the danger from to*o* much speed. Gravel may ~~coarse~~ *cause* you to skid and crash, or an oil slick can send you over the edge.

~~Remembering~~ *I remember* my most exciting skateboard experience as if it were yesterday. *T*here was a steep and winding road that zig-zagged down a hill. Fortunately, I managed to zoom around all the curves in a breath-taking ride from top to bottom. ~~Talk about~~ *What* a thrill!

A good ~~technick~~ *technique* for picking up speed for a leap and turn in mid-air is to propel your~~selve~~ *self* with your right foot. *T*hen kick o*f**f* for the leaping turn from the ground.

I will always remember my first skateboard tube. It was situated in a park ~~and All~~ my friends were ~~their~~ *there* to cheer me on as I spun the ~~weels~~ *wheels* of my skateboard with my hands and listened to the ballbearings whizz. Then I ~~new~~ *knew* that I was always going to have an exciting time skateboarding.

REPORTS

A report is an informative piece of writing. It is written to give an accurate factual account of an event or situation. A good report is clearly written, well laid out and presents the facts in a logical manner. Although it is impersonal, the author's opinions or recommendations may be included at the end.

You may be asked to write a report on the annual sports day, the school drama, activities in your local club, an event you witnessed, a survey you carried out, the school tour, and so on.

When you write a report you should:
- Give the report a title and date
- Open with a summary statement (give a single sentence describing the problem/event etc.)
- Present the information:
  - what happened
  - where it happened
  - when it happened
  - why it happened
  - how it happened
  - who was present

    OR
  - state the problem
  - outline the causes
  - describe the consequences
  - give the solutions

    OR
  - state the terms of the report
  - describe the research carried out
  - outline the results

- Present all of the facts
- Be accurate
- Always use:
  - clear language
  - precise descriptions
  - short sentences

- separate paragraphs for each aspect of the report
- headings or sub-headings if appropriate
- Avoid slang and too many technical terms
- End with your opinions or recommendations
- Sign the report

Here are three different types of reports. The first is a report on a school tour, the second is about the destruction of the ozone layer, and the third is a report related to a survey carried out by students in their school.

This report is about an event.

Structure

Title: The School Tour

Date: 1st October 20____

Summary statement

Who
What
Where
When

On Friday, 1st October, our class went on a school trip to Kilkenny.

Detailed information in the body of the report

Our coach left the school car park at 8.30am. Our first stop was at the Dunmore Caves. Our guide led us down a steep flight of steps to the underground caverns and pointed out the stalagmites, stalactites and the pillars. She said it was the darkest place in Ireland. Then she switched the lights off. We could not see a thing. She told us that women, children and babies who hid in the caverns had been slaughtered by the Vikings when they attacked Kilkenny. Later the caverns were used by a woman who came to worship the devil. We were all relieved when she turned the lights on again so that we could find our way to the exit.

At the visitor centre there was a collection of objects found in the area when the caverns were opened. They included a leather bag of coins dropped by one of the Vikings when he attacked the Irish people in the underground cave.

At 11.30am we went to Kilkenny Castle and had a tour of the main rooms and the art gallery. We then had one hour for lunch. We were allowed to have a picnic lunch in the castle grounds or go to a restaurant.

At 2.00pm we visited Rothe House, a museum for everyday objects from medieval times onwards. Later we walked to St. Canice's Cathedral and saw the round tower built by the monks where they stored their goods and could watch out for the Vikings.

We had half an hour to shop or go for something to eat before we boarded the coach at 4pm. We arrived back at the school at 6 o'clock.

RECOMMENDATIONS

Our class felt that it was a very good trip. The guided tour of the Dunmore Caves was the highlight of the day. However, it would have been a good idea to do some activity, such as bowling, rather than visit so many historical sites.

Recommendations/
Assessment

There was not enough time to shop or to have lunch.

Most students would have liked to spend a longer time in Kilkenny and to have stayed overnight.

Signed:

Signature — Aoife Byrne

Here is a report about a problem.

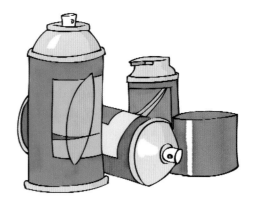

Title: Destruction Of the Ozone Layer

Date: 18th January 20_____

The earth's ozone layer has been getting thinner since the middle of the twentieth century. Ozone is a form of oxygen found in the atmosphere 10km to 30km above the surface of the planet. It has protected life on earth from the sun's harmful ultraviolet (UV) rays. Ozone is being destroyed six times faster than nature can replace it.

> Structure
> Problem

Damage to the ozone layer is caused by man-made chemicals such as chlorofluorocarbons (CFCs) and halons. Halons are used in fire extinguishers. CFCs are found in a range of products including aerosols, foam used in food packaging, coolants in refrigerators and air conditioners.

> Causes

Destruction of the ozone layer means that more UV radiation reaches the earth's surface. UV radiation results in eye problems and increased rates of skin cancer. Scientists believe that 1 per cent less ozone causes up to 6 per cent more skin cancers. UV radiation also damages crops growing in fields and affects sea life.

> Consequences

Ozone destruction is a global problem. All countries must work together to reduce the production of CFCs. Ireland has agreed with the rest of the EU to eliminate CFCs by the beginning of this century. Individuals can help by buying ozone friendly products.

> Solutions

Signed:

Kieran Doyle

> Signature

This is a report that is based on the results of a survey.

Title: A Survey of Litter Problems in Our School

Date: 14th November 20_____

Terms: A survey of the litter problem in our school, requested by the school principal, was carried out by the Student Council so as to create a new policy on litter prevention for the school.

Research: The Student Council drew up a questionnaire on the litter problem and distributed it to each class. It was completed by students during form class.

Results: • 60% stated there was a serious or very serious problem with litter in the school
           • 30% thought it was a problem
           • 5% stated it was not a problem
           • 5% had no opinion

           An analysis of litter in the classrooms revealed that
           • 45% was waste paper
           • 30% was tins and bottles
           • 20% was crisp bags and plastic wrappings
           • 3% was cartons
           • 2% other

           When asked to identify the causes of the problem
           • 70% stated a lack of bins
           • 20% stated not enough cleaning staff
           • 8% stated laziness
           • 2% did not know

Conclusion: There is a serious litter problem throughout the school. Litter was found in every classroom in the building.

Recommendations: Recycling bins could be provided for bottles, cans, cartons and paper. Ordinary bins could be provided for other waste. The school could run an awareness campaign to highlight the issue. Management could employ more cleaners.

Signed:

Eileen Finn
Chairperson

YOUR TURN

Write a report on two of the following topics:

- A visit to your school by a famous person
- A talk to your class by a recovering drug addict
- The greenhouse effect
- Students smoking in your school
- The school sports day
- Changes students would like to see in the school tuck shop

DIARIES

Anne Frank, a young Jewish girl, lived in Amsterdam during World War II. In 1942, when she was thirteen years old, the Franks went into hiding to escape from the Nazis. They lived in cramped quarters in the upper back rooms of an old building where her father had worked. The entrance to their new home was hidden behind a bookcase. Anne confided her thoughts and feelings to 'Kitty' — a diary she had received on her thirteenth birthday. She made her first entry on Sunday, 14 June, 1942 and her last one on Tuesday, 1 August, 1944. Three days later the hiding place was discovered. The family was arrested and sent to the concentration camps. Anne died in Bergen-Belsen concentration camp in March, 1945. The diary, which had been left behind during the raid on the building, was published after the war.

These two entries, written early in 1943, show how difficult it was for Anne to cope with the strain of living in a confined space with her mother, father and sister, and the other families who lived secretly on the upper floors, while the war raged outside.

Wednesday, 13 January, 1943

Dear Kitty,

Everything has upset me again this morning, so I wasn't able to finish a single thing properly.

It is terrible outside. Day and night more of those poor miserable people are being dragged off, with nothing but a rucksack and a little money. On the way they are deprived even of these possessions. Families are torn apart, the men, women and children all being separated. Children coming home from school find that their parents have disappeared. Women return from shopping to find their homes shut up and their families gone.

The Dutch people are anxious too, their sons are being sent to Germany. Everyone is afraid.

And every night hundreds of planes fly over Holland and go to German towns, where the earth is ploughed up by their bombs, and every hour hundreds and thousands of people are killed in Russia and Africa. No one is able to keep out of it, the whole globe is waging war and although it is going better for the Allies, the end is not yet in sight.

Saturday, 30 January 1943

Dearest Kitty,

I'm seething with rage, yet I can't show it. I'd like to scream, stamp my foot, give Mother a good shaking, cry and I don't know what else because of the nasty words, mocking looks and accusations that she hurls at me day after day, piercing me like arrows from a tightly strung bow, which are nearly impossible to pull from my body. I'd like to scream at Mother, Margot, the Van Daans, Dussel and Father too: 'Leave me alone, let me have at least one night when I don't cry myself to sleep with my eyes burning and my head pounding. Let me get away, away from everything, away from this world!' But I can't do that. I can't let them see my doubts, or the wounds they've inflicted on me. I couldn't bear their sympathy or their good-humoured derision. It would only make me want to scream even more.

Everyone thinks I'm showing off when I talk, ridiculous when I'm silent, insolent when I answer, cunning when I have a good idea, lazy when I'm tired, selfish when I eat one bite more than I should, stupid, cowardly, calculating, etc., etc. All day long I hear nothing but what an exasperating child I am, and although I laugh it off and pretend not to mind, I do mind. I wish I could ask God to give me another personality, one that doesn't antagonise everyone.

But that's impossible. I'm stuck with the character I was born with, and yet I'm sure I'm not a bad person. I do my best to please everyone, more than they'd ever suspect in a million years. When I'm upstairs, I try to laugh it off because I don't want them to see my troubles.

More than once, after a series of absurd reproaches, I've snapped at Mother: 'I don't care what you say. Why don't you just wash your hands of me? – I'm a hopeless case.' Of course, she'd tell me not to talk back and virtually ignore me for two days. Then suddenly all would be forgotten and she'd treat me like everyone else.

It's impossible for me to be all smiles one day and venomous the next. I'd rather choose the golden mean, which isn't so golden, and keep my thoughts to myself. Perhaps sometime I'll treat the others with the same contempt as they treat me. Oh, if only I could.

Yours, Anne

From *The Diary of Anne Frank*

EXPLORING THE TEXT

1 What has upset Anne, according to the diary entry of 13 January, 1943?

2 Has her mood changed by 30 January, 1943? In what way?

3 Why do people think she is 'an exasperating child'?

4 How does she respond to their accusations?

5 Which of the diary entries do you prefer? Explain your choice.

6 Imagine you are living in the same building as Anne. Write your impression of her.

YOUR TURN

WRITE A DIARY ENTRY

Imagine you are one of the people below and write a diary entry. In your account, mention a series of events, when and where they happened, your role and who else was there at the time.

- **Street kid**
- **Taxi driver**
- **Pop star**
- **Teacher**
- **Criminal**
- **Fire fighter**
- **Politician**
- **Millionaire**
- **Waiter**
- **Astronaut**
- **Lifesaver**
- **Pet cat**
- **Ghost**

A REVIEW

A review is a response to a novel, poem, play, film, or any other creative work. Most reviews contain:
• An introduction
• A summary of the piece under review
• An assessment of the piece, or a recommendation

A book review should include the following:
• The title
• The name of the author
• The name of the publisher
• The number of pages in the book
• An introduction
• Setting or location
• Main characters
• Plot summary (do not give away the ending!)
• Themes
• Style of writing/language
• What you liked/disliked about the book
• Overall assessment/recommendation

Look at this review of John Quinn's novel *The Gold Cross of Killadoo.*

THE GOLD CROSS OF KILLADOO

Title: *The Gold Cross of Killadoo*
Author: John Quinn
Publisher: Poolbeg
Number of pages: 106 pages

Introduction

John Quinn is a well-known writer. His first work of fiction for young people, *The Gold Summer of Lily and Esme*, won the Irish Children's Book Trust Bisto Book of the Year 1992. This novel is an equally good read.

Setting, main characters and plot summary

The Gold Cross of Killadoo is set in Ireland during the summer of AD 990. Derval and her brother Eoin are visiting Killadoo monastery when the Vikings attack and steal a priceless, newly-made cross along with other valuables they find. Eoin and Derval are captured by the ruthless invaders and brought to Dublin by their leader, One-Eyed Leif, to be sold as slaves. Leif expects to make a handsome profit from their sale, but he underestimates the determination of the feisty Derval and her courageous brother to escape from Dublin and return the cross to the monks at Killadoo. The story follows the adventures of the two young Irish captives as they encounter a wide variety of characters in the Viking stronghold, including Leif's future bride, Helga, the blind youth Daithi Dall and a Norse-Irish family living in the city.

Use of present tense in the review

Assessment

This is a fast-moving, exciting and action-packed novel that provides fascinating insights into life in tenth century Ireland. The broad range of interesting and entertaining characters engage the reader's attention and sympathy, while the many humorous incidents and the strong storyline make this a thoroughly enjoyable read.

Recommendation

This is one of the best novels I have come across recently and I would recommend it highly as a work of teenage fiction.

1 In the introduction, what do we learn about the author?
2 In the summary, what two locations are mentioned?
3 What crisis occurs at the monastery?
4 Where are the children taken? Why?
5 According to the review, what qualities make this novel interesting?

FILM REVIEW

This is a review of the popular film *Babe*. The main character in this film is a pig with the power of speech.

BABE

Who would have thought we could find a hero in a piglet? He's courageous, determined, naive and vulnerable.

Babe's tale is simple. He's won in a raffle and taken home to the Hoggett farm run by Farmer Hoggett (James Cromwell) and his wife (Magda Szubanski) where he is provisionally adopted by two border collie sheep dogs. Babe is resourceful and learns new skills at being a 'sheepdog'. The sheep take a shine to him because they are tired of being nipped and growled at and Babe speaks to them politely unlike the bullying sheepdogs. However, looming is the constant threat of Babe becoming Christmas dinner, but Ferdinand, the wise-cracking duck, serves as a mischievous distraction.

One would like to believe the complete surprise success at the box office of this film is attributed to the tender goodness and charm of its hero. But the

other engaging factor was the enchanting magical illusion created by the animals that talk to each other. 'The animal characters are so real that I felt we could best serve the story by using live animals; animation was never considered,' explains producer and co-writer George Miller (of the *Mad Max* series).

For the inaugural leading role pigs were trained by hand via coddling, nurturing and TLC at just two weeks old, and filming started at 16 to 18 weeks before they lost their optimal cuteness. 'Every three weeks we'd start a new group so they'd be prepared when the preceding group outgrew its usefulness,' explained Miller. In all, 48 pigs appeared on screen as Babe.

Jim Henson's Creature Shop created special anatomical clones for facial expressions of the lead animals and computer-aided graphic images for talking. 'It's by far the toughest job we've ever done,' said Neil Scanlan, head of Henson's 16-person crew.

The film is honest enough to show that life on the farm can be painful or sad for the animals, but these aspects are not dwelled upon and do not ruin the freshness of this entertaining family comedy.

EXPLORING THE TEXT

1 In the introduction to this response, what do we learn about the qualities possessed by the main character, Babe?

2 In the second paragraph the film's plot is summarised. Why is the word 'sheepdog' in inverted commas?

3 Why was the film a 'complete surprise success'?

4 Why were live animals used in the film?

5 Why did they need to use more than one pig for Babe?

6 In what way does the writer feel that the film is honest about life on the farm?

7 What do you think is the writer's opinion of the film?

8 After reading this response, would you go and see Babe? Why or why not?

YOUR OPINION

Write a review of one of the following:

- **A film you enjoyed**
- **A book you read**
- **A poem you liked**
- **A painting that appealed to you**
- **A sculpture that impressed you**
- **Any other piece of creative work that you either loved or hated**

INSTRUCTIONS

The purpose of instructions is to show how something can or should be done. Most texts usually include:

- An introduction in which the aim of the instructions is given
- The objects that are involved in the instructions
- A series of steps showing the order in which the instructions are to be performed.

Let's look at the structure and language features of a typical set of instructions: a recipe.

HOW TO MAKE SHORTBREAD

Cooking time   20–25 minutes
Cooking utensil   greased oven tray
Ingredients

1¼ cups flour
1 tablespoon rice flour
2 tablespoons caster sugar
½ cup butter
½ teaspoon vanilla essence

Method

1 Set oven at 160°C.
2 Sift flours, add sugar and rub in butter. Add vanilla. Work into a stiff dough. Turn on to a lightly floured board and knead well.
3 Divide mixture into three or four. Roll each into a circle 1 cm thick and the size of a saucer. Pinch edges. Lift on to oven tray. Cut each round into 8 pieces and mark with fork.
4 Bake at 160°C until pale fawn colour – 20–25 minutes.

5 Cool on cake cooler.

- **Write out instructions for the following on a page:**
  - **how to put on a coat**
  - **how to tie your shoelaces**

Give the page to the student next to you and see whether he or she can successfully complete the tasks, based on your instructions only! For the purpose of this exercise, assume that your classmate has never seen a coat or a shoe before.

- **Write out the rules for your favourite game.**

EXPLANATION

The purpose of an explanation is to tell how or why things or events work or occur. Most explanations are organised to include:

- A general statement that introduces the thing or event – this can be in the form of a question, for example, 'How does a car engine work?'
- A series of statements that describe how or why something works, including its parts or components
- A concluding statement that sums up the explanation

Let's look at the structure and language features of a typical explanation.

HOW CAN SNAKES MOVE WITHOUT LEGS?

Snakes can crawl and slither over every kind of surface – yet they have no legs.

A snake's backbone is very flexible and supports many ribs. Muscles that attach the tips of the ribs to broad scales on the snake's belly allow a snake to move each scale separately.

The snake's ribs act as legs while the scales act as feet. As the snake glides, twists and turns, its scales move against projections such as pebbles and push it forward, often very swiftly and smoothly. Strangely enough, the fossil remains of snakes show that they once possessed real legs.

YOUR TURN

HOW TO . . .

Try writing an explanation of your own. Choose one of the following activities and explain how to do it. Share your explanation with other class members.

Explain how to . . .

• Pitch a tent

• Play tennis

• Make a cake

• Ride a bicycle

- Clean up your room
- Drive a car
  - Ride a horse
    - Swim
  - Ski
  - Make friends
  - Cook your favourite meal
    - Repair a leaking tap
    - Ride a skateboard
    - Care for a pet
    - Sail a boat
    - Play basketball
  - Train a dog
- Take a photograph
- Pass exams
- Do a magic trick
- Build a tree house

CHAPTER 9

ADJECTIVES AND ADVERBS

WHAT YOU WILL LEARN IN THIS CHAPTER

- How to bring your writing alive by using adjectives and adverbs
- The effect of adjectives in different types of texts
- Adjectives you can add to your vocabulary

HOW YOU WILL LEARN

- Identifying adjectives and adverbs in different contexts
- Exploring the use of adjectives and adverbs in texts
- Creating adjective portraits and advertisements

ADJECTIVES

Adjectives are describing words – they add colour and meaning to our world and paint detailed word pictures. We use adjectives to create colours, shapes, sizes, feelings and other qualities in nouns. Writers use adjectives to make their writing come alive and to give the reader more details about people, places, feelings and things.

Adjectives tell us what kind.

gigantic *clumsy*
dangerous

For example: The lion is a **wild** animal.

Adjectives tell us how many.

ten *one*
five *none*

For example: There are **six** trains to the national park.

Adjectives point out.

this *those*
these *the*
that

For example: **These** people are famous.

Adjectives tell how much.

much *enough*
some *whole*

For example: There was **much** disappointment when the party was cancelled.

Adjectives tell us what colour.

red *amber*
green *blue*

For example: The **green** light is showing.

YOUR TURN

ADJECTIVES IN ADVERTISING

People all around us – novelists, poets, advertisers, cartoonists and many others – use adjectives to give insight into life.

In the car advertisement below, notice how adjectives are used to begin the advertisement to focus our attention on the qualities and appearance of the car: *Small, Nimble, Useable, Quick.*

Read through the advertisement, then complete the grid using adjectives of your own to describe the car.

[The CRX has *it.*]

Small. Nimble. Useable. *Quick.* And very single minded; one driver, one passenger, their luggage. No baggage. Just sensations in the tips of your fingers and the seat of your pants. *It's* waiting for you. At just $39,990*.

Telephone: 1800 672 217 Web www.honda.com.au *Recommended retail price, spoiler optional. Excludes dealer delivery and statutory charges. HCC3174/2

FEATURES	YOUR ADJECTIVES
Colour	....
Size	....
Speed	....
Appearance	....
Wheels	....
Road	....

In the following description of a bird of prey, the novelist has used adjectives to add interest and detail to the description.

THE EAGLE

The bird hung in the air above the river. It was so low that Luke could see it clearly, a **big nuggetty** bird with **strong** talons and a **curving** beak. Its feathers were **beautiful** – a **lovely chestnut** colour on the back and sides, and **bright white** on the head and breast. The wing-tips were **black**.

From *Brahminy* by Colin Thiele

A girl and the way she is dressed are beautifully described, using many adjectives, in this extract from the novel *Hating Alison Ashley* by Robin Klein.

ALISON

She was wearing this soft blue skirt, and a shirt the colour of cream, with not a crease nor a wrinkle nor a loose thread anywhere. Expensive-looking plaited leather sandals. Long, pale gold hair caught back with a filigree clasp, and tiny gold roses, the size of shirt buttons, in her ears. Her skin was tanned and each cheek had a deep, soft dimple. Huge navy-blue eyes, the colour of ink, fringed with dark curly lashes. She was the most beautiful, graceful, elegant thing you ever saw in your life.

From *Hating Alison Ashley* by Robin Klein

1 Identify the adjectives that describe the following aspects of the girl's dress and appearance:

Skirt _____

Hair _____

Roses _____

Eyes _____

Lashes _____

Dimples _____

2 Which are the three adjectives used to describe the overall impression of the girl?

J.R.R. Tolkien skilfully uses adjectives to create the weird appearance of the goblins in his novel *The Hobbit*.

THE GOBLINS

There in the shadows on a large flat stone sat a tremendous goblin with a huge head, and armed goblins were standing round him carrying the axes and the bent swords that they use. Now goblins are cruel, wicked, and bad-hearted. They make no beautiful things, but they make many clever ones. They can tunnel and mine as well as any but the most skilled dwarves, when they take the trouble, though they are usually untidy and dirty.

From *The Hobbit* by J.R.R. Tolkien

1 Which adjectives describe the size and shape of the stone on which the largest goblin sits?

2 Which adjectives are used to describe the goblin's size and head?

3 What is the shape of the goblins' swords?

4 Which adjectives does the writer use to describe the goblins' character?

5 Which are the two adjectives that describe the goblins' unusual appearance?

FORMING ADJECTIVES

Form adjectives from the words in brackets to complete the phrases below. The first one has been done to help you.

1 A *comfortable* lounge (comfort)
2 An. . . . . attempt (hero)
3 A . . . . sunset (gold)
4 A . . . . experiment (science)
5 A . . . . painting (beauty)
6 A . . . . parrot (talk)
7 An . . . . dog (affection)
8 A . . . . mother (pride)
9 An . . . . game (energy)
10 An . . . . teacher (anger)
11 A . . . . swimmer (fame)
12 A . . . . rescue (courage)
13 A . . . . summer (heat)
14 A . . . . investigation (crime)
15 A . . . . prize (marvel)
16 A . . . . effort (strength)
17 A . . . . ornament (value)
18 A . . . . illness (mystery)
19 A . . . . tree (giant)
20 A . . . . poem (sense)

USING ADJECTIVES TO DESCRIBE THINGS

Food, glorious food!

Think of an adjective to go with each of the following foods. The first one has been done to help you.

1 baked potatoes
2 . . . . rice
3 . . . . coffee
4 . . . . cheese
5 . . . . cake
6 . . . . fruit salad

USING BETTER ADJECTIVES

You must be careful in your use of some adjectives because, if you use the same ones too often, they can lose their vitality. The poet Judith Nicholls has written a poem about the overworked adjective.

NICE WORK

Never use the word NICE, our teacher said.
It doesn't mean a thing!
Try . . .
beautiful, shining, delicious,
shimmering, hopeful, auspicious,
attractive, unusual, nutritious –
the choice is as long as a string!
But please, *never use the word NICE,*
it just doesn't mean a thing!
(She's nice, our teacher.)

Judith Nicholls

REPLACING NICE

Replace *nice* in each of the following sentences with a better adjective from the box.

friendly	comfortable	cooling	refreshing	fertile
delicious	picturesque	sunny	thrilling	energetic

1 We went for a *nice* swim in the pool.
2 It was a *nice* day.
3 He owns a *nice* dog.
4 They played a *nice* game of tennis.
5 The bed was very *nice*.
6 We had a *nice* view.
7 There was a *nice* breeze.
8 They ate a *nice* meal.
9 He read a *nice* detective novel.
10 The farm has *nice* soil.

CREATE YOUR OWN ADVERTISEMENT

Create your own advertisement for one of the following products using the materials listed, pay special attention to the use of adjectives.

Materials
- Cut-outs from magazines
- Your own drawings
- Your own advertising copy

Products
- Car
- Roller blades
- Mountain bike
- Television quiz show
- Restaurant
- Pet food
- Favourite food
- Soft drink
- Sporting event
- Theme park
- Special effects film
- Kitchen gadget

ADVERBS

As their name suggests, adverbs add meaning to verbs. They are also used to add meaning to adjectives and other adverbs.

You can usually identify a word as an adverb by testing to see whether it answers the questions *how? when?* or *where?* with regard to a verb, or *to what extent?* with regard to an adjective or another adverb.

ADVERBS TELL HOW

I swung **slowly** from side to side as my parachute floated **smoothly** towards the earth.

ADVERBS TELL WHEN

A few minutes **earlier** I had been standing in the plane. **Soon** my feet would touch the ground.

ADVERBS TELL WHERE

I turned **around** as I drifted **down** and saw the most beautiful clouds.

ADVERBS TELL HOW MUCH OR TO WHAT EXTENT

I had been **very** nervous before I jumped but I became **totally** calm after my chute opened. I **quite** often think about that exciting time.

IDENTIFYING ADVERBS

Write down the adverbs in the following advertisement. Most, but not all, of these adverbs end in 'ly'.

VISIT DOLPHIN COVE

Dolphins swim swiftly, dive gracefully, surface suddenly, live beautifully and sing softly to each other under the waves. Travel now with Eco Tours to Dolphin Cove.

Live simply yet comfortably in a climate that is always summer. Come away to Dolphin Cove and closely observe nature.

Eat exquisitely cooked meals, dress casually, walk lazily along the rainforest paths, sleep soundly in a grass hut and ride the waves proudly with the creatures that exist harmoniously with nature – the dolphins.

Novelists use adverbs to increase the interest level of their writing and to vary their writing style. Look how the writers of the following extracts from novels have used adverbs.

ADVERBS IN NOVELS

GILLY HOPKINS

Galadriel Hopkins shifted her bubble gum to the front of her mouth and began to blow **gently**. She blew until she could **barely** see the shape of the social worker's head through the pink bubble.

From *The Great Gilly Hopkins* by Katherine Paterson

THE SEARCH

Suddenly, **frantically,** he went through his pockets, dived to the floor, looked under the table and under his chair, shot up again, scanned the table, pounced on the bowl of cereal.

From *This School is Driving Me Crazy* by Nat Hentoff

THE HEADMASTER'S DOG

From the first I knew it mightn't **necessarily** be my kind of school. We came whamming up the drive at about ninety K and **nearly** ran over a small round object that I **later** found out was the Headmaster's dog.

It looked like a hairy speed bump.

When I **eventually** met the Headmaster I could see the connection, except he was bald.

From *The Great Gatenby* by John Marsden

ADVERB STORIES

Complete the following stories by using the correct adverbs from the boxes in the spaces.

skilfully	frantically	badly
soon	below	heavily
quietly	loudly	menacingly

BREAK IN!

The intruder forced the door open and crept .... into the house. He .... found the safe and .... worked out the combination. But the alarm sounded .... and a dog growled .... As the intruder ran .... to the window, he cut himself .... in his attempt to escape. He fell .... onto the lawn. The police who were waiting .... grabbed him and hustled him into a waiting car.

mercilessly	accidentally	cautiously
confidently	miraculously	
helplessly	early	

RESCUE!

.... in the morning, the yacht had .... hit a reef and was floundering .... in the huge waves that were .... pounding the yacht against the rocks. As a sea rescue craft .... approached the wreck, one woman who had .... survived, dived into the sea and swam .... towards her rescuers.

CHAPTER 10

POETRY

- The structure of different poems including ballads, free verse, lyrics, sonnets, limericks, acrostic poems, shape poems
- The words used to describe and analyse poems

- Reading examples of different poems and discussing them, either as a class or in groups
- Recording your responses to a variety of poems
- Writing your own poems

INTRODUCTION TO POETRY

There are poems about everything: happiness, sadness, loneliness, companionship, dogs, cats, nature, cities, love, hate, life and death. Reading poems can be very enjoyable. Many poems have something important to say. They make you think. Robert Frost, an American poet, wrote that 'poetry begins in delight and ends in wisdom'. The English critic Matthew Arnold said that poetry is 'the most beautiful, impressive and wisely effective mode of saying things'.

Poems can be written in a number of different forms, including ballad, free verse, sonnet, song lyric, haiku, limerick, elegy and ode. Poets are able to choose an appropriate poetic form to express their feelings and ideas. For example, the ballad is appropriate for the telling of a story; the free verse form allows the development of a poetic theme without the discipline of strict rhyme and rhythm; the sonnet is a poem of fourteen lines usually expressing a fixed idea; the song lyric is a form that is often set to music; the haiku is ideal for the expression of a single glimpse of life.

There are also a number of other simple poetic forms such as the shape poem, the acrostic, the cinquain and others that the poet can use to entertain the reader.

POETRY

What is Poetry? Who knows?
Not the rose, but the scent of the rose;
Not the sky, but the light in the sky;
Not the fly, but the gleam of the fly;
Not the sea, but the sound of the sea;
Not myself, but what makes me
See, hear, and feel something that prose
Cannot; and what it is, who knows?

Eleanor Farjeon

Here is a list of keywords to help you discuss a poem.

Alliteration The repetition of the same consonants (letters that are not vowels), usually at the beginning of words that are close together in the line.

Assonance The repetition of a vowel (a, e, i, o, u) or a vowel sound, in words that are close together.

Atmosphere The sensations linked to a place or time.
a gloomy house
a cheerful room
a spooky castle

Blank verse Verse that does not rhyme.

Free verse The poem does not follow fixed poetic rules. The number of lines and their length and the shape of the poem vary.

Image	A picture that is created in the mind of the reader, e.g. 'a red rose'. To create images the poet uses metaphors, similes and personification.
Lyric	A short poem that describes an emotion or emotions. The language in a lyric is simple yet musical.
Metaphor	A comparison that does not use the words 'like', 'as' or 'than'. *The sea is a hungry dog.*
Mood	The feeling in the poem. It can be happy, sad, hopeful, angry and so on.
Onomatopoeia	The use of words that sound like their meaning. 'Buzz', 'tinkle', 'splash', 'squelch'
Personification	This occurs when human qualities are given to non-human things. *The sun smiled down on the happy children.* *The wind sighed through the trees.*

Rhythm	The beat of the line.
Run-on-lines	When a sentence continues from one line to the next. Also known as enjambment.
Similes	A comparison using the words 'like', 'as' or 'than'.
	Her skin was like ice.
	Her skin was as cold as ice.
	Her skin was colder than ice.
Stanza	The verse.
Symbol	A symbol represents something else. A heart is used to represent love. A dove is used to represent peace.
Theme	The central idea in the poem.
	Bullying may scar a person for life.
Tone	The sound of the poem or the speaker's voice in the poem. It can be happy, sad, frightened, regretful, triumphant and so on. The tone may change in the poem. It often matches the mood.

You can use these terms to discuss any of the poems you are about to read.

FREE VERSE

Many modern poets write what is called free verse. Free verse does not have a structured pattern of rhyme and rhythm. It has flexibility because it does not follow strict rules. It does have a rhythm, which is created by the natural flow of the poet's thoughts and emotions. As the term 'free verse' suggests, the poet no longer has to keep to a regular pattern. There is far more freedom and less artificiality.

In this poem, the choice of a free verse form allows the poet, Carol-Anne Marsh, to express the sadness of parting with more freedom than a rigid framework of rhyme and rhythm would allow.

GOODBYE

He said
goodbye.
I shuffled
my feet
and kept a close
watch on my
shoes.

He was talking
I was listening
but he probably
thought I was
not
because I never
even lifted my
head.

I didn't want him
to see
the mess mascara
makes when it
runs.

Carol-Anne Marsh

THE SONNET

The sonnet is a lyric poem that has fourteen lines. It first appeared in Italy in the thirteenth century. If you look at the line endings of 'Magpies', you'll see that this poem, like many sonnets, has an alternating rhyme scheme. Sonnets usually have a 'turning point' at the end of the eighth line.

MAGPIES

Along the road the magpies walk
with hands in pockets, left and right.
They tilt their heads, and stroll and talk.
In their well-fitted black and white
they look like certain gentlemen
who seem most nonchalant and wise
until their meal is served and then
what clashing beaks, what greedy eyes!

But not one man that I have heard
throws back his head in such a song
of grace and praise – no man nor bird.
Their greed is brief; their joy is long.
For each is born with such a throat
as thanks his God with every note.

Judith Wright

EXPLORING THE TEXT

1 What is the setting of the poem?
2 How does the poet show that magpies are like people?
3 What is the 'well-fitted black and white' of the magpies?
4 How do the magpies act when their meal is served?
5 What special gift do the magpies have?

6   What do the songs of the magpie consist of?

7   What does the poet suggest the magpies are doing in every note of their song?

8   What do you think is the poet's purpose in this poem?

9   Why is this poem classed as a sonnet?

10 Did you enjoy reading this poem? Why or why not?

HAIKU

Haiku is a Japanese verse form that aims to capture in words a delightful moment from the world of nature. Basho, a famous seventeenth-century Japanese haiku poet, said a haiku should set out to 'capture a vision into the nature of the world'.

A typical haiku has three lines with a total of seventeen syllables. See how a haiku is set out by reading some of the haikus below. Then, using them as models, try to create haikus of your own.

Line 1 5 syllables
Line 2 7 syllables
Line 3 5 syllables

LITTLE FROG

Little frog among
rain-shaken leaves, are you, too,
splashed with green paint?

Gaki

HAIKU

Flashing neon night
blurred through a steamy window:
a concert of colours!

James W. Hackett

PLAYGROUND HAIKU

Everyone says our
playground is overcrowded
but I feel lonely.

Helen Dunmore

WILD GEESE

Going yesterday
Today, tonight . . . the wild geese
Have all gone, honking.

Taniguchi Buson

LIMERICKS

Limericks are funny little poems that you can have a lot of enjoyment reading and writing. They are made up of five lines. The longer first, second and fifth lines rhyme with each other. The third line rhymes with the fourth line.

Generally the last line of the limerick contains a surprise. A limerick often begins with the words, 'There was a. . .' and ends with the punch line.

A GREEDY YOUNG MAIDEN NAMED FIRKINS

A greedy young maiden named Firkins
Would recklessly gorge on raw gherkins
Till one day on a spree
She consumed eighty-three
And pickled her innermost workin's.

SOMETIMES EVEN PARENTS WIN

There was a young lady from Gloucester
Who complained that her parents both bossed her,
So she ran off to Maine.
Did her parents complain?
Not at all – they were glad to have lost her.

THE SMILE ON THE FACE OF THE TIGER

There was a young lady from Niger
Who smiled as she rode on a tiger.
They returned from the ride
With the lady inside,
And the smile on the face of the tiger.

ACROSTIC POEMS

Acrostic poems are fun to write. First of all, choose the title of your poem. It can be any subject you like. For example: food, cars, happiness, holidays, parents, friends and sport. Write the letters of your title down the page and then create your poem. Here are two acrostic poems that will give you the idea.

SPIDER

Spinning webs to catch its prey
Pincers waving in anticipation
In and out of hiding
Dropping off a silvery rope
Edging closer, sensing movement
Ready for dinner

Allison Reldas

FOREST

Full of the sounds of insects and birds
Often bursting with leaves
Restlessly alive
Earthscape of green canopies
Slanting light through branches
Trees

Allison Reldas

SHAPE POEMS

Shape poems are poems created in the same shape as their subjects. The shape of the poem immediately shows the reader what the poem is about. Here is a shape poem for you to read, enjoy and think about.

A CELLO

My
cello big and fat
makes
the sound
of a screeching
rat. It plays F
double sharp
when I want
it to play
B flat. It
sounds like
a bad com-
position when
I play in the 4th
position. If I try
to play vibrato my
bow goes all
s-t-a-c-c-
ato
!

Richard Lester

SCHOOL DAYS

- Do you remember your first day in junior school? Write an account of it and share it with the class. If you cannot remember all the details, someone in your family may be able to help you. How old were you? Who went with you – an older brother, sister or friend, a parent? How did you feel? Do you recall what you did? What were you wearing? What time did you return home?
- What the best thing that happened to you during your time in junior school?
- What was the funniest thing that occurred when you were in school? You may like to tell the class but do not embarrass another student.
- What was the worst thing that happened to you in school?
- Interview an older person about his or her first day in school. Was it like your first day? How was it the same? In what way was it different? If you get permission, record the interview and play it to the class. Remember to prepare for the interview. Write out your questions before hand, ask them and then give the interviewee time to respond!

These poems are written about different aspects of school life.

TICH MILLER

Tich Miller wore glasses
with elastoplast pink frames
and had one foot three sizes larger than the other.

When they picked teams for outdoor games
She and I were always the last two
left standing by the wire-mesh fence.
We avoided one another's eyes,

Stooping, perhaps to re-tie a shoelace,
or affecting interest in the flight

of some unfortunate bird, and pretended
not to hear the urgent conference:
"Have Tubby!" "No, no, have Tich!"

Usually they chose me, the lesser dud,
and she lolloped, unselected,
to the back of the other team.

At eleven we went to different schools.
In time I learned to get my own back,
sneering at hockey players who couldn't spell.

Tich died when she was twelve.

Wendy Cope

EXPLORING THE TEXT

1 Comment on the name 'Tich'. Is it a glamorous name? What does it suggest about the girl?

2 Describe Tich Miller's appearance.

3 What do the girls do while waiting to be picked? Why?

4 Comment on the name 'Tubby'.

5 The word 'lolloped' is used in the fifth stanza. Repeat it aloud slowly three or four times. What is the effect of the word? What kind of movement is it attempting to capture?

6 The poem is written in stanzas of three lines. Why is the last line left on its own?

7 Write the theme (central message) of this poem in one or two sentences.

8 What are the feelings of the speaker in the poem? Support the points you make by referring to and quoting from the text.

THE BOY WITHOUT A NAME

I remember him clearly
And it was thirty years ago or more:
A boy without a name.

A friendless, silent boy,
His face blotched red and flaking raw,
His expression, infinitely sad.

Some kind of eczema
It was, I now suppose,
The rusty iron mask he wore.
But in those days we confidently swore
It was from playing near dustbins
And handling broken eggshells.

His hands, of course, and knees
Were similarly scabbed and cracked and dry.
The rest of him we never saw.

They said it wasn't catching: still, we knew
And strained away from him along the corridor,
Sharing a ruler only under protest.

I remember the others: Brian Evans,
Trevor Darby, Dorothy Cutler.
And the teachers: Mrs Palmer, Mr Waugh.

I remember Albert, who collected buttons.
And Amos, frothing his milk up with a straw.
But his name, no, for it was never used.

I need a time-machine.
I must get back to nineteen fifty-four
And play with him, or talk, at least.

For now I often wake to see
His ordinary, haunting face, his flaw.
I hope his mother loved him.

Oh, children, don't be crueller than you need.
The faces that you spit on or ignore
Will get you in the end.

Allan Ahlberg

1 Why was the boy unhappy? He was 'infinitely sad'. What is the significance of the word 'infinitely'?

2 The speaker in the poem wants to go back in time. What are his reasons?

3 'I hope his mother loved him'. Can you suggest why the speaker wishes this?

4 What advice does the speaker give in the final stanza?

5 What is the mood of this poem? Is it sad, regretful, angry, or something else? Where is it most evident?

6 How does the speaker feel now about the way the boy was treated? Refer to and quote from the poem to support your point of view.

7 What does the poet mean by the line 'The faces that you spit on or ignore will get you in the end.'?

8 Give your response to this poem. Do you like or dislike it? Do you think that it has an important point to make? How does it make you feel? Have you ever experienced anything similar?

9 Read 'The Loner' by Julie Holder. Which of the two poems did you prefer? Why?

10 Imagine you are the speaker in this poem. You enter a time machine and return to 1954. You meet the boy in the school. Write out what happens.

THE LONER

He leans against the playground wall,
Smacks his hands against the bricks
And other boredom-beating tricks.
Traces patterns with his feet.
Scuffs to make the tarmac squeak,
Back against the wall he stays
And never plays.

The playground's quick with life,
The beat is strong.
Though sharp as a knife
Strife doesn't last long.
There is shouting, laughter, song,
And a place at the wall
For who won't belong.

We pass him running, skipping, walking.

In a slow huddled groups, low talking.
Each in our familiar clique
We pass him by and never speak,
His loneliness is his shell and shield
And neither he nor we will yield.

He wasn't there at the wall today,
Someone said he'd moved away
To another school and place
And on the wall where he used to lean
Someone had chalked 'watch this space'.

Julie Holder

1 Where is 'The Loner' set?

2 What does the boy do? Why does he not play?

3 How to the other children react to him?

4 What do you think is meant by the line 'His loneliness is his shell and shield'?

5 In your opinion, why did he move to another school?

6 From your reading of the poem, describe the loner's feelings as he leans against the wall.

7 'Watch this space'. Why did someone chalk these words on the wall?

8 What does the poem tell us about children?

9 What line or lines made the greatest impression on you? Explain your choice.

10 Imagine you are the loner. Write a diary entry about your experience of life in school.

Dreamed I was in a school playground,
    I was about four feet high
Yes dreamed I was back in the playground,
    and standing about four feet high
The playground was three miles long and the
    playground was five miles wide
It was broken black tarmac with a high fence
    all around
Broken black dusty tarmac with a high fence
    running all around
And it had a special name to it, they called it
    The Killing Ground.

Got a mother and a father, they're a thousand miles away
The Rulers of the Killing Ground are coming out to play
Everyone thinking: who they going to play with today

    You get it for being Jewish
    Get it for being black
    Get it for being chicken
    Get it for fighting back
    You get it for being big and fat
    Get it for being small
    Oh those who get it get it and get it
    For any damn thing at all

Sometimes they take a beetle, tear off its six legs one by one
Beetle on its black back rocking in the lunchtime sun
But a beetle can't beg for mercy, a beetle's not half the fun
Heard a deep voice talking, it had that iceberg sound
'It prepares them for life' – but I have never found
Any place in my life that's worse than the Killing Ground.

Adrian Mitchell

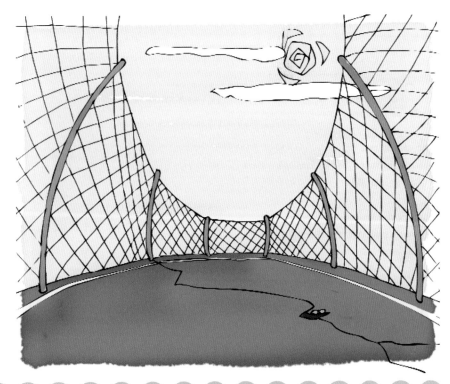

EXPLORING THE TEXT

1 Jot down three words you would normally use to describe a playground. What words do the children use in 'Back in the Playground Blues'? Why?

2 Why does the poet still dream about the playground?

3 Examine the description of the playground. What strikes you as unusual?

4 Why are the children bullied?

5 What is the difference between the child and the beetle from the bully's point of view?

6 Does the attitude of the adults surprise you? Why?

7 The poet uses repetition in the poem. What is the effect of this repetition?

8 Comment on the title of the poem. What other title would you give it, if you had a choice?

9 Write down the main theme of the poem. Are there other themes also? What are they?

10 Write a letter to the school principal, complaining that your child has been bullied in the playground during break time. Describe what happened and suggest some solutions to the problem.

FIGHT

'A scrap! A scrap!'
The tingle in the scalp
starts us running.

The shout drains
our playground just as though
a plug was pulled

here in the space
in which two twisted, furious
bodies writhe.

Rules will not prise
these savages apart.
No ref will interpose

with shouts of 'Break!'
This contest has one single
vicious round

of grab and grapple,
wrestle, thump and scrabble,
flail and scratch.

We take no sides.
Our yells are wolves howling
for blood of any kind.

Our fingers clench.
The thrill claws in our throats
like raging thirst.
The whistle shrills
and splits our pack. The circle
heaves and shatters.

The fighters still
are blind and deaf, won't hear
or see until,

parted, they go limp
as cubs drawn by the scruff
from some hot lair.

Now they are tame,
Standing outside Sir's room
grinning their shame.

Chastened, we feel
the snarls of wildness
stifle in us.

Barrie Wade

EXPLORING THE TEXT

1 Explain in your own words what happens in the poem.

2 Identify a metaphor in 'Fight'. In your opinion, why did the poet use this particular image?

3 Choose a sentence in the poem that you liked and explain your choice.

4 What is the meaning of the last stanza?

5 In groups of four, draw up a set of rules about behaviour in the school grounds during break-time. Appoint one of the group to take notes and one to read the rules to the class. Write the rules on the blackboard and discuss which ones would be most effective.

TEACHER

Summer beckons,
jostles the girls
who stare at a poem.

I'm done with them,
weary of their battle
for the warm whip of the sun,
straining to live what they read.

Blameless, of course.
Who could be still
and not anguished, giddy,

as drifts of blossom
eddy outside like pink snow?
Soon there'll be prizes, goodbyes.
I shall become again

the half-remembered voice
from a place of imprisonment,
a rudiment of chalk and red ink,

shall inhabit a cupboard
in someone's mind,
locked in the past as they ascend
inert and adult asylums.

Mary E. O'Donnell

EXPLORING THE TEXT

1 Who is speaking in this poem?
2 Where and when is the poem set?
3 Does the teacher blame the students for 'straining to live what they read'? Quote from the poem to support your answer.
4 How does the teacher expect to be remembered by the students?
5 Is this the teacher's first experience of teaching? How do you know?

6 What type of future does the teacher foresee for the students?

7 Having read the poem, describe the mood of the teacher. Refer to the poem to support your answer.

8 Does the teacher's attitude surprise you? Explain your answer.

9 Choose an image you felt was effective and briefly explain your choice.

10 Write a poem or essay about school life from a teacher's point of view.

THE NATURAL WORLD

TIME TO THINK

- If you were given a choice, would you live in the country or the city? Jot down the advantages of life in the country and life in the city. Discuss them with the person beside you.
- What is your favourite season? Why? Design a poster of your favourite season. Include all the things that you like about that time of year. Put your name on it and hang it on the classroom wall.
- What season do you like the least? Why? Suggest four things you could do to make the season more enjoyable.
- Write down a list of the sounds you associate with your favourite season. Compare them with your classmates' lists.

Now read the following poems and discover how poets have been inspired by the natural world.

WHAT IS . . . THE SUN?

The sun is an orange dinghy
    sailing across a calm sea.

It is a gold coin
    dropped down a drain in heaven.

It is a yellow beach ball
    kicked high into the summer sky.

It is a red thumb-print
    on a sheet of pale blue paper.

It is the gold top from a milk bottle
    floating on a puddle

Wes Magee

1 This is a poem based on metaphors. Choose the metaphor you liked the most and explain your choice.

2 Comment on the poet's use of colour.

3 Using this poem as a model, write your own poem 'What is the Moon'? Put it on a large sheet of paper and hang it in your classroom.

This anonymous Irish poem was written between the seventh and thirteenth centuries. The vivid images of winter are typical of early Irish poetry.

MY STORY

Here's my story; the stag cries,
Winter snarls as summer dies.

The wind bullies the low sun
In poor light; the seas moan.

Shapeless bracken is turning red,
The wildgoose raises its desperate head.

Birds' wings freeze where fields are hoary.
The world is ice. That's my story.

Version: Brendan Kennelly

EXPLORING THE TEXT

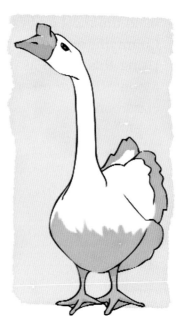

1 List all the verbs used in this poem.
2 How important are the verbs in creating a wintry atmosphere?
3 Suggest another title for the poem and explain your choice.
4 Write a short poem of four rhymed couplets on the pleasant things about winter.

WINTER

The winter trees like great sweep's brushes
Poke up from deep earth, black and bare,
Suddenly stir, and shake a crowd
Of sooty rooks into the air.

L.A.G. Strong

EXPLORING THE TEXT

1 Write out the simile in this poem. Is it an effective one? Why?

2 In what sense are rooks 'sooty'? Did the poet choose this word for another reason also? Explain your answer.

3 What is the dominant (main) colour in the poem? Why did the poet decide to use this colour?

4 Compare 'My Story' and 'Winter'. Which poem did you prefer? Why?

I WANDERED LONELY AS A CLOUD

I wandered lonely as a cloud
That floats on high o'er vales and hills,
When all at once I saw a crowd,
A host, of golden daffodils;
Beside the lake, beneath the trees,
Fluttering and dancing in the breeze.

Continuous as the stars that shine
And twinkle on the Milky Way,
They stretched in never-ending line
Along the margin of a bay;
Ten thousand saw I at a glance,
Tossing their heads in sprightly dance.

The waves beside them danced; but they
Outdid the sparkling waves in glee:
A poet could not but be gay,
In such a jocund company:
I gazed – and gazed – but little thought
What wealth the show to me had brought:

For oft, when on my couch I lie
In vacant or in pensive mood,
They flash upon that inward eye
Which is the bliss of solitude;
And then my heart with pleasure fills,
And dances with the daffodils.

William Wordsworth

1   What is the simile in the opening stanza? Do you think it is effective? Why?

2   What is the difference between the mood of the poet and the flowers?

3   What is the effect of the word 'golden'?

4   What simile is used in the second stanza? Why did Wordsworth use it, in your opinion?

5   Were there really ten thousand daffodils? Explain your answer.

6   In the third stanza, what change occurs? What causes the change?

7   In the first and last stanza the poet is alone. Does he feel the same in both stanzas? What has happened?

8   Wordsworth uses personification in the poem. Select three examples of personification and state which one you liked the best. Explain your choice.

9   What is the theme of this poem? Refer to the text in your answer.

10 Write a passage about an event (real or imaginary) that suddenly changed your mood.

THE TREES

The trees are coming into leaf
Like something almost being said:
The recent buds relax and spread,
Their greenness is a kind of grief.

Is it that they are born again
And we grow old? No, they die too.
Their yearly trick of looking new
Is written down in rings of grain.

Yet still the unresting castles thresh
In fullgrown thickness every May.
Last year is dead, they seem to say,
Begin afresh, afresh, afresh.

Philip Larkin

EXPLORING THE TEXT

1 In which season is this poem set? Explain your choice.
2 How do the trees renew themselves?
3 What does the poet mean when he describes the trees as 'unresting castles'?
4 Find an example of onomatopoeia in this poem. What sound is the poet trying to capture? What letters make this sound? Read this poem aloud to hear the full effect of the word.
5 What is the theme of 'The Trees'? Quote from the poem to support your answer.

THISTLES

Against the rubber tongues of cows and the hoeing
hands of men
Thistles spike the summer air
Or crackle open under a blue-black pressure.

Every one a revengeful burst
Of resurrection, a grasped fistful
Of splintered weapons and Icelandic frost thrust up

From the underground stain of a decayed Viking.
They are like pale hair and the gutturals of dialects.
Every one manages a plume of blood

Then they grow grey, like men.
Mown down, it is a feud. Their sons appear,
Stiff with weapons, fighting back over the same
ground.

Ted Hughes

●●●● EXPLORING THE TEXT ●●●●

1 When do thistles bloom?

2 Who are their enemies?

3 Write down the words and images in this poem that are associated with fighting and warriors.

4 Why does the poet compare the thistle to a Viking?

5 According to Hughes, what happens when thistles are mown down?

6 Who wins the war?

7 Discuss the poet's attitude towards the plant. Does he admire it, fear it or hate it?

8 Choose your favourite image from the poem and explain why you liked it.

9 Did you enjoy reading this poem? Give reasons for your answer.

10 Look up thistles in an encyclopaedia or on the Internet and write a short passage about them.

BLACKBERRY-PICKING

Late August, given heavy rain and sun
For a full week, the blackberries would ripen.
At first, just one, a glossy purple clot
Among others, red, green, hard as a knot.
You ate the first one and its flesh was sweet
Like thickened wine: summer's blood was in it
Leaving stains upon the tongue and lust for
Picking. Then the red ones inked up and that hunger
Sent us out with milk-cans, pea-tins, jam-pots
Where briars scratched and wet grass bleached our boots.
Round hayfields, cornfields and potato-drills
We trekked and picked until the cans were full,
Until the tinkling bottom had been covered
With green ones, and on top big dark blobs burned
Like a plate of eyes. Our hands were peppered
With thorn pricks, our palms sticky as Bluebeard's.

We hoarded the fresh berries in the byre.
But when the bath was filled we found a fur,
A rat-grey fungus, glutting on our cache.
The juice was stinking too. Once off the bush
The fruit fermented, the sweet flesh would turn sour.
I always felt like crying. It wasn't fair
That all the lovely canfuls smelt of rot.
Each year I hoped they'd keep, knew they would not.

Seamus Heaney

EXPLORING THE TEXT

1 When and where is this poem set?

2 What causes the blackberries to ripen?

3 Choose a metaphor you liked in this poem and briefly explain why you thought it was good.

4 The poem appeals to our senses. Give an example of each one you find.

5 Find an example of onomatopoeia in the poem. Which letters create the sound? Why does the poet use onomatopoeia?

6 Images of blood are found throughout the poem. Trace these images and state why you think Seamus Heaney uses them.

7 Comment on the use of the word 'hoarded'.

8 What is the theme of the poem?

9 Trace the changes of mood and tone in this poem.

10 Research the story of Bluebeard in your library or on the Internet and read your account to the class.

THE SEA IS A HUNGRY DOG

The sea is a hungry dog,
Giant and grey.
He rolls on the beach all day.
With his clashing teeth and shaggy jaws
Hour upon hour he gnaws
The rumbling, tumbling stones,
And 'Bones, bones, bones, bones!'
The giant sea-dog moans,
Licking his greasy paws.

And when the night wind roars
And the moon rocks in the stormy cloud,
He bounds to his feet and snuffs and sniffs,
Shaking his wet sides over the cliffs,
And howls and hollos long and loud.

But on quiet days in May or June,
When even the grasses on the dune
Play no more their reedy tune,
With his head between his paws
He lies on the sandy shores
So quiet, so quiet, he scarcely snores.

James Reeves

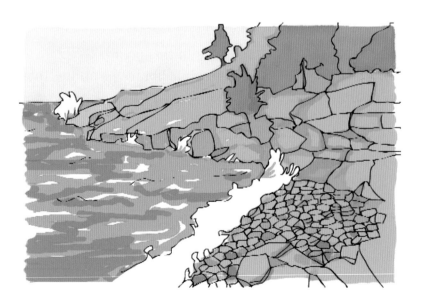

1 In what way does the sea act like a dog, according to the poet? Quote from the poem to support your answer.

2 What is the difference between the way the sea behaves during the day and at night?

3 The sea is different in May or June. How do you know?

4 Read the poem aloud. What is the mood of the sea? Listen to the tone of your voice to help you decide.

5 Do you find the comparison between the sea and a hungry dog an interesting one? Why or why not?

6 When the poet says that the sea is a hungry dog is he using a simile or a metaphor?

7 The poet uses onomatopoeia to capture the sounds that the sea makes. How many 'sea' sounds can you find in the poem? Write out the lines where they occur. For each example you use, state what letters create the sound.

8 Choose one image from the poem that you particularly liked and explain your choice.

9 Did you enjoy reading this poem? Why or why not?

10 Compose your own poem using an interesting comparison.

FAMILIES

• Do you have brothers and sisters? Are they older or younger than you? What are the advantages and what are the disadvantages of having siblings?

• If you do not have brothers and sisters, what are the advantages of being the only child? What do you least like about not having siblings?

• In groups of four, decide on six rules parents should follow when raising children. Share your ideas with the rest of the class.

- Think of a painful accident (a wasp sting, a fall, or a more serious incident) that you have experienced. Tell the person beside you what happened. Describe how you felt. How did your family react?
- Recount your happiest memory connected with your family. It can be something very important, such as a wedding, or something very small.

Here are some poems that are based upon memories of family events and that examine the relationships between different family members.

I SEE YOU DANCING, FATHER

No sooner downstairs after the night's rest
And in the door
Than you started to dance a step
In the middle of the kitchen floor.

And as you danced
You whistled.
You made your own music
Always in tune with yourself.

Well, nearly always, anyway.
You're buried now
In Lislaughtin Abbey
And whenever I think of you

I go back beyond the old man
Mind and body broken
To find the unbroken man.
It is the moment before the dance begins,

Your lips are enjoying themselves
Whistling an air.
Whatever happens or cannot happen
In the time I have to spare
I see you dancing, father.

Brendan Kennelly

1 The poet speaks directly to 'you' in the poem. Who is the person?

2 What is the poet's favourite memory of his father?

3 What did the father do as he danced?

4 How did he change as he grew older?

5 What happened to him at the end?

6 From your reading of the poem, what type of man was the father?

7 Explain in your own words the lines
       'You made your own music
       Always in tune with yourself.'

8 Having read the poem, do you think that you would have liked the father? Give reasons for your answer.

9 Write down the image you liked most in this poem and explain briefly why you liked it.

10 Write a poem about one of your relatives.

NETTLES

My son aged three fell in the nettle bed.
'Bed' seemed a curious name for those green spears,
That regiment of spite behind the shed:
It was no place for rest. With sobs and tears
The boy came seeking comfort and I saw
White blisters beaded on his tender skin.
We soothed him till his pain was not so raw.
At last he offered us a watery grin,
And then I took my hook and honed the blade
And went outside and slashed in fury with it
Till not a nettle in that fierce parade
Stood upright any more. Next task: I lit
A funeral pyre to burn the fallen dead.
But in two weeks the busy sun and rain
Had called up tall recruits behind the shed;
My son would often feel sharp wounds again.

Vernon Scannell

• • • • EXPLORING THE TEXT • • • •

1 How old was the boy?

2 Why does the poet give his age?

3 *'Bed' seems a curious name for a place where the nettles grew.* Do you agree? Explain your answer.

4 Describe in your own words what happened to the little boy?

5 What did the father do? How did he feel? When are his feelings shown most clearly?

6 What do you think the poet means by the final line?

7 Jot down as many words linked with fighting and soldiers that you can find in the poem. Why does the poet use these words?

8 What is the theme of the poem?

9 What do you learn about the way the father feels about the son?

10 Read the poem through from beginning to end. Now read the poem Thistles (page 221). In what ways are they similar? How are they different? Which do you prefer and why?

MID-TERM BREAK

I sat all morning in the college sick bay
Counting bells knelling classes to a close.
At two o'clock our neighbours drove me home.

In the porch I met my father crying –
He had always taken funerals in his stride –
And Big Jim Evans saying it was a hard blow.

The baby cooed and laughed and rocked the pram
When I came in, and I was embarrassed
By older men standing up to shake my hand

And tell me they were 'sorry for my trouble'.
Whispers informed strangers I was the eldest,
Away at school, as my mother held my hand

In hers and coughed out angry tearless sighs.
At ten o'clock the ambulance arrived
With the corpse, stanched and bandaged by the nurses.

Next morning I went up into the room. Snowdrops
And candles soothed the bedside; I saw him
For the first time in six weeks. Paler now,

Wearing a poppy bruise on his left temple,
He lay in the four foot box as his cot.
No gaudy scars, the bumper knocked him clear.

A four foot box, a box for every year.

Seamus Heaney

EXPLORING THE TEXT

First stanza

1 What words do you normally think of when someone mentions your mid-term break?

2 Where did the child sit all morning? Was he ill?

3 Comment on the use of the word 'knelling'. What word is normally used? Does the word hint at what the poem is about?

4 What else is strange about the events in the first stanza?

Second Stanza

5 Does the father normally cry at funerals?

Third Stanza

6 Do old men usually stand up when children enter a room?

Fourth Stanza

7 What do we learn in this stanza?

Fifth Stanza

8 Contrast the mother's reaction to the father's. Did it surprise you?

9 What is the usual function of an ambulance?

Sixth Stanza

10 In your opinion, why did the boy not go to see the corpse immediately?

11 What does he look at when he goes into the room? What does he look at afterwards? Why?

12 Comment on the use of the word 'soothed'.

13 How long has it been since he was last home?

14 Explain in your own words what has happened in the meantime.

General Questions

15 Based on your reading of this poem, what is the boy's attitude to death? Does it change at any point? Why?

16 Choose an image you think is particularly effective and explain your choice.

17 Why is the final line left on its own?

18 What is the tone of the last seven lines? How does the poet achieve this effect? Comment on his use of assonance and alliteration.

19 In this poem, everything is turned upside down: the student is in sick bay although he is well; the father cries; the old men stand up when the young boy enters the room and so on. Why does Heaney give us these details? What has caused the normal order to be overthrown? Is it a reflection of the theme?

20 Write your own poem based on the title 'Mid-Term Break'. It must be an original effort and should not include details from Heaney's poem.

MOTHER OF THE GROOM

What she remembers
Is his glistening back
In the bath, his small boots
In the ring of boots at her feet.

Hands in her voided lap
She hears a daughter welcomed.
It's as if he kicked when lifted
And slipped her soapy hold.

Once soap would ease off
The wedding ring
That's bedded forever now
In her clapping hand.

Seamus Heaney

EXPLORING THE TEXT

1 What does the mother remember when her son is getting married?

2 How does she feel?

3 What does she do?

4 Rewrite the poem under the title 'Father of the Groom.'

WHEN ALL THE OTHERS

When all the others were away at Mass
I was all hers as we peeled potatoes.
They broke the silence, let fall one by one
Like solder weeping off the soldering iron:
Cold comforts set between us, things to share
Gleaming in a bucket of clean water.
And again let fall. Little pleasant splashes
From each other's work would bring us to our senses.

So while the parish priest at her bedside
Went hammer and tongs at the prayers for the dying
And some were responding and some crying
I remembered her head bent towards my head,
Her breath in mine, our fluent dipping knives –
Never closer the whole rest of our lives.

Seamus Heaney

EXPLORING THE TEXT

1 What form of poem is this? How do you know?

2 What did the child and the mother do, when everyone had gone to Mass?

3 They did not speak. Was it an unpleasant silence? Explain your answer.

4 What is the contrast in the sestet (six lines)?

5 What does the poet remember most clearly?

6 What is the theme of this poem?

FROM A SEQUENCE OF POEMS FOR MY DAUGHTER

IV

When you were young,
You took the love I gave you
And gave me all you had,
Held nothing back.
Things were easier then.
Now, twelve years from the womb
You face me:
　'This is what I am,' you say,
　'This is who I am.
　You gave me life (a dubious gift –
　double-edged, welcome and
　unwelcome),
Now you have to live with me.'

Well, that is so,
And we are bound as inextricably to
each other
As if the birthcord had never been cut,
pulling and pushing.
Why did I think it would be easy?

V

I love you –
Child of my womb
Child of my heart
Pain-bringer
Love-giver
Joy-maker
Time-taker
Heart-healer
Daughter mine.

Debi Hinton

EXPLORING THE TEXT

Stanza IV

1　Describe the relationship between the mother and daughter when the daughter was a baby.

2　How old is her daughter now?

3　Has the relationship changed? How? Refer to the poem in your answer.

4　How does the mother feel about their relationship now? Where is this evident?

5　What is your response to this poem?

Stanza V

1　How does the mother feel about her daughter?

2　What does the child bring into the mother's life?

3　What does she take away from the mother?

4　If you were asked to give this poem a title, what would it be? Explain your choice.

FROM THE PATTERN

Little has come down to me of hers,
a sewing machine, a wedding band,
a clutch of photos, the sting of her hand
across my face in one of our wars

when we had grown bitter and apart.
Some say that's the fate of the eldest daughter.
I wish now she'd lasted till after
I'd grown up. We might have made a new start

as women without tags like *mother, wife,*
sister, daughter, taken our chances from there.
At forty-two she headed for god knows where.
I've never gone back to visit her grave.

Paula Meehan

●●●●● EXPLORING THE TEXT ●●●●●

1 The mother has left a number of things to her daughter. What are they?

2 What was the relationship between them? Where is this most obvious in your opinion?

3 What do we learn about the mother from the poem?

4 What do we learn about the daughter?

5 Why does the daughter wish her mother had lived longer, according to the poem?

6 What do you understand by the line
'At forty-two she headed for god knows where'.

7 Suggest reasons why the girl never visited her grave.

8 Read the poem aloud. What is the tone – happy, sad regretful or wistful?

9 Give your response to this poem.

10 Have you a special relationship with someone in your family (a grandparent, aunt, uncle, parent, brother, sister, cousin)? Describe the relationship and explain why it is so special.

MYSTERY

TIME TO THINK

- Write out the plot of the scariest story you know and read it to your class.
- Interview an older person about fairy stories or ghost stories he or she remembers. You may like to record the interview and play it to your class, but remember to ask permission first!
- Tell the person beside you a ghost story. When you are finished, he or she will tell the story to the class.

Now enjoy these poems written about mysterious people and places.

When we moved to Miller's End,
Every afternoon at four
A thin shadow of a shade
Quavered through the garden-door.

Dressed in black from top to toe
And a veil about her head
To us all it seemed as though
She came walking from the dead.

With a basket on her arm
Through the hedge-gap she would pass,
Never a mark that we could spy
On the flagstones or the grass.

When we told the garden-boy
How we saw the phantom glide,
With a grin his face was bright
As the pool he stood beside.

'That's no ghost-walk,' Billy said,
'Nor a ghost you fear to stop –
Only old Miss Wickerby
On a short cut to the shop.'

So next day we lay in wait,
Passed a civil time of day,
Said how pleased we were she came
Daily down our garden-way.

Suddenly her cheek it paled,
Turned, as quick, from ice to flame.
'Tell me,' said Miss Wickerby.
'Who spoke of me, and my name?'

'Bill the garden-boy.'
She sighed,
Said, 'Of course, you could not know
How he drowned – that very pool –
A frozen winter – long ago.'

Charles Causley

1. Describe the appearance of the old woman.
2. What did the children think she was?
3. Who did they tell?
4. What was his response?
5. Who was the real ghost?
6. How did he die?
7. Were you surprised by the ending?
8. Is the ghost a typical one? Explain your answer.
9. 'Suddenly her cheek it paled,
   Turned as quick, from ice to flame.'
   Is this a simile or a metaphor? Explain your answer.
10. Write a story about the death of Bill and why his ghost haunts the pool.

EMPTY FEARS

What's that? – Coming after me, down the street,
With the sound of somebody dragging one foot
Behind him, who pauses, who watches, who goes
With a shuffle and mutter
From the wall to the gutter
In the patch where the light from the lamps doesn't meet . . .

Oh . . . it's only a bit of paper – a hollow brown bag
Open-mouthed, like a shout – a bit like the face
Crumpled-up, of someone who's going to cry,
Blown on the wind, from place to place,
Pointless, and light, and dry.

Who's that? – Watching, from the upstairs windows
Of the house where the hedge grows right back to the door,
Where the half-drawn curtains droop and discolour
And a yellow bulb burns away
And the milk's on the step all day –
Somebody lives there, no one comes or goes . . .

Oh . . . it's only an empty coat on a hanger
That sways in a draught like a man who depends
On only one thing – the something inside
That's holding him up, waiting for friends
He writes to, but no one's replied.

What's that? – Whispering, where the fence round the lot
Sags like a fading hope: the gate just here twists
On its hinge like a bird's broken wing
And shrieks as you look, and see:
Nothing, where all the shops used to be,
People coming and going where now they are not . . .

Oh . . . it's only the breeze that's fretting itself
Amongst the stiff thistles, each standing alone,
Upright, all winter, dead, but not gone . . .

But if it's only these things, what blows
Through me, to make me afraid, who knows?

Brian Lee

1 The speaker fears three things in this poem. What are they?

2 What sounds does he fear? What causes them?

3 What sight terrifies him?

4 How does he feel when he asks the question at the beginning of the stanza? How does he feel when he says 'Oh . . .'?

5 Where is the setting? Is it in his room, at school, in the street, on a bridge? How do you know?

6 What time of the day and year is it? Give reasons for your answer.

7 What is the atmosphere in the poem? Where is it most evident?

8 Choose two similes you like from the poem and state why you think that they are effective.

9 What do you think the poet means by the last lines?

10 Write your own poem about your worst fear.

MIDNIGHT WOOD

Dark in the wood the shadows stir:
What do you see? –
Mist and moonlight, star and cloud,
Hunchback shapes that creep and crowd
From tree to tree.

Dark in the wood a thin wind calls:
What do you hear? –
Frond and fern and clutching grass
Snigger at you as you pass,
Whispering fear.

Dark in the wood a river flows:
What does it hide? –
Otter, water-rat, old tin can,
Bones of fish and bones of a man
Drift in its tide.

Dark in the wood the owlets shriek:
What do they cry? –
Choose between the wood and river;
Who comes here is lost for ever,
And must die!

Raymond Wilson

EXPLORING THE TEXT

1 Where and when is the poem set?

2 How does the setting help to create an atmosphere?

3 What is there to fear in the wood?

4 Find one example of personification in the poem. Do you think that it is effective? Why?

5 Read 'Midnight Wood' aloud. What sounds are there in the poem? Are they friendly or threatening? How did the poet create these sounds?

FLANNAN ISLE

'Though three men dwell on Flannan Isle
To keep the lamp alight,
As we steer'd under the lee, we caught
No glimmer through the night.'

A passing ship at dawn had brought
The news; and quickly we set sail,
To find out what strange thing might ail
The keepers of the deep-sea light.

The winter day broke blue and bright,
With glancing sun and glancing spray,
As o'er the swell our boat made way,
As gallant as a gull in flight.

But, as we near'd the lonely Isle,
And look'd up at the naked height;
And saw the lighthouse towering white,
With blinded lantern, that all night
had never shot a spark
Of comfort through the dark,
So ghostly in the cold sunlight
It seem'd, that we were struck the while
With wonder all too deep for words.

And, as into the tiny creek
We stole beneath the hanging crag,
We saw three queer, black, ugly birds –
Too big, by far, in my belief,
For guillemot or shag –
Like seamen sitting bolt-upright
Upon a half-tide reef:
But, as we near'd, they plunged from sight,
Without a sound, or spurt of white.

And still too 'mazed to speak,
We landed; and made fast the boat;
And climb'd the track in single file,
Each wishing he was safe afloat,
On any sea, however far,
So it be far from Flannan Isle:

And still we seem'd to climb, and climb,
As though we'd lost all count of time,
And so must climb for evermore.
Yet all too soon, we reached the door –
The black, sun-blister'd lighthouse-door,
That gaped for us ajar.

As, on the threshold, for a spell,
We paused, we seem'd to breathe the smell
Of limewash and of tar,
Familiar as our daily breath,
As though 'twere some strange scent of death:
And so, yet wondering, side by side,
We stood a moment, still tongue-tied:
And each with black foreboding eyed
The door, ere we should fling it wide,
To leave the sunlight for the gloom:
Till, plucking courage up, at last,
Hard on each other's heels we pass'd
Into the living-room.

Yet, as we crowded through the door,
We only saw a table, spread
For dinner, meat and cheese and bread;
But all untouch'd; and no one there:
As though, when they sat down to eat,
Ere they could even taste,
Alarm had come; and they in haste
Had risen and left the bread and meat:
For at the table-head a chair
Lay tumbled on the floor.
We listen'd; but we only heard
The feeble chirping of a bird
That starved upon its perch:
And, listening still, without a word,
We set about our hopeless search.

We hunted high, we hunted low,
And soon ransack'd the empty house;
Then o'er the Island, to and fro,
We ranged, to listen and to look
In every cranny, cleft or nook
That might have hid a bird or mouse:
But, though we search'd from shore to shore,
We found no sign in any place:
And soon again stood face to face
Before the gaping door:
And stole into the room once more
As frighten'd children steal.

Aye: though we hunted high and low,
And hunted everywhere,
Of the three men's fate we found no trace
Of any kind in any place,
But a door ajar, and an untouch'd meal,
And an overtoppled chair.

We seem'd to stand for an endless while,
Though still no word said,
Three men alive on Flannan Isle,
We thought on three men dead.

W.W. Gibson

● ● ● ● EXPLORING THE TEXT ● ● ● ●

1 How many men lived on Flannan Isle?

2 What was their work?

3 Why did the rescuers sail out to the island?

4 The mood of the men changed as they neared the island. What caused this change of mood?

5 What did the speaker notice about the three birds as they landed? What did the birds do?

6 Why did the men not rush in to the lighthouse?

7 What did they see when they entered the room?

8 Did they find the men or any clue as to why they disappeared?

9 Read the poem through again. What possibly happened to the men on Flannan Isle? Base your answer on evidence in the poem only.

10 Write a story based on what you think happened on Flannan Isle.

CHAPTER 11

DRAMA

WHAT YOU WILL LEARN IN THIS CHAPTER

- The origins of European drama
- The difference between comedy, tragedy and mime
- How to write a play

HOW YOU WILL LEARN

- Reading a short history of drama
- Studying extracts from plays
- Performing scenes for your class
- Writing your own play based on a short story

INTRODUCING DRAMA

Drama, as we know it today, had its origins in Greece. The plays were performed outdoors, in huge amphitheatres. Some of these theatres could hold up to 35,000 people. There were no special effects, curtains or stage props and there was little scenery or lighting. The actors wore eye-catching costumes and used masks. Occasionally one actor played two or more parts. The female roles were played by young men, as women were not allowed to perform.

Over time, two kinds of plays became popular – tragedies and comedies. The tragedy has a sad ending. The main character looses everything that is important to him. He is often responsible for his own downfall, though fate also acts against him. The comedy, on the other hand, has a happy ending. All misunderstandings are cleared up, the hero and heroine are reunited and everyone lives happily ever after.

One form of comedy is called farce. It is based on stereotypical characters, e.g. the typical Frenchman, Italian, Irishman and blonde. There is usually much confusion and misunderstanding before everything works out at the end. *King Chicken* is a farce. The playwright assumes you know about the main characters – Tarzan and

Jane, Stanley and Livingstone. The characters are not realistic, the plot is silly and the jokes obvious. Farces are great fun and should not be taken seriously.

Mime is a form of drama where the actors use gestures, expressions and actions to communicate with the audience. They do not use words. The golden rule in mime is 'show, don't tell'.

In this chapter you will have the opportunity to read examples of comedy and tragedy and take part in drama exercises.

SHOW TIME

MIME

Choose one of the scenes below and mime it for your class. Do not tell which one you have chosen and do not use props!

- An impatient man is waiting at a bus stop and an elderly woman comes along with two heavy shopping bags.
- A parent scolding a guilty child.
- Two students trying to pass a note during class.
- Two friends have fallen out and are not talking to each other.
- Two supporters of different teams at a match. One team scores.
- A student trying to eat crisps during class.
- A person returning home, searching for a set of house keys.
- Two hikers attempting to hitch a lift from passing cars.
- A clumsy person trying to hang a picture on a wall.

CONTRAST AND CONFLICT

The best drama often arises from conflict between contrasting characters. Choose one of the following scenes and perform it with a friend. You may write out the dialogue and rehearse the scene before hand if you wish, or you can stand up and improvise.

- A teenage son comes home wearing an earring. His father objects. The son refuses to remove it. He argues that he has the right to wear what he likes. His father does not agree.
- A parent comes home early, smells cigarette smoke and accuses the teenage son/daughter of smoking. The teenager denies it.
- A teenager wants to go to a party in a friend's house. His/her mother suspects that there will not be any adults present. She refuses permission. They have an argument.
- A teenager decides to take the day off school while his parents are on a business trip. He tries to persuade his best friend to join him. They disagree.
- Two teenagers are sitting in the sitting room. One is a serious student and wants to work. The other is very untidy and wants to talk.
- Two women go into a café. One is very easy going. The other is critical and very fussy, especially about hygiene.
- A husband and wife have won a shopping voucher to be used in a huge shopping complex. She wants to buy a new washing machine. He wants a new set of golf clubs.

Now that you have performed your own plays, it is time to enjoy extracts from three popular dramas.

COMEDY

KING CHICKEN

INTRODUCTION

King Chicken is pure farce. It is often stated that farce is only worthwhile when it carries a moral message, that is when the laughter is directed against the more outrageous of man's activities and beliefs. Therefore one may be tempted to see in this play a comment on the white man abroad in 'unenlightened' countries. That may be so, but the play's main aim is one of simple humour through absurdity.

Every role should be overacted in the best traditions of farce, with every actor doing his best to upstage and out-act the rest of the cast, using grandiose movements of arms and legs and exaggerated tones of voice.

CAST

Bottomley (English Explorer)
Stanley (English Explorer)
Jane
Tarzan

SCENE

Deepest Africa, last century. A jungle clearing with a big rock centre stage. Bottomley and Stanley are crouched behind the rock, looking fearfully off.

Bottomley:	End of the line for us, Stanley old friend, end of the line! Surrounded on all sides by a herd of raging elephants out for our good British blood!
Stanley:	Buck up, Bottomley – we'll fight to the last bitter drop!
Bottomley:	But how, man how? Our guns are empty, you've sprained your ankle and I've caught jungle malaria that's slowly driving me insane. It's no use! We're finished! The last hunt!
Stanley:	Bit of a tough spot, I must admit. Still, we can look on the bright side.
Bottomley:	What bright side? We're trapped and there's no way out!
Stanley:	I don't suppose we'll ever find Doctor Livingstone now. Six months we've been searching this cursed jungle, looking behind every tree, in every bush, under every stone, and now...
Bottomley:	To finish our lives squashed flat under the foot of a charging elephant! What a horrible way to die – it's ... it's so ... un-British!
Stanley:	Come, come, Bottomley, don't go to pieces.
Bottomley:	A poor joke, old man, under the circumstances.
Stanley:	Forgive me, old friend – just trying to cheer you up.
Bottomley:	Cheer me up, he says! My heavens, how Myrtle will mourn for me! Ah, my dear wife ... if only I could see her smiling face once more. And what of little Norton and tiny Matilda? Left – without a father! How heartbreaking –
Stanley:	You can't give in, Bottomley. Remember that an Englishman never says die, never! It's simply not done! Whatever would they say about you back at the club?
Bottomley:	What does it matter, Stanley? It's over! *(He looks off).* The elephants are coming closer, closer! I can hear the thunder of their charge! I can almost see the whites of their eyes!
Stanley:	Then let us at least die like proud and brave sons of old England!
Bottomley:	How?

Stanley:	Screaming for mercy. Help! Someone! Anyone!

(Jane comes bounding in. She is dressed in animal skins.)

Jane:	Hullo, big white bwanas.
Bottomley:	Stanley, someone heard us!
Jane:	Whole jungle hear you.
Stanley:	Great Scott – it's a woman . . . I think.
Jane:	Me Jane.

(Both men rise and face her.)

Stanley:	How do you do, Miss . . . er . . . I'm sorry, I didn't catch the last name.
Jane:	Me Jane. Me Tarzan's woman. You heard of Tarzan?
Bottomley:	Tarzan? I don't believe it!
Jane:	Why not? This only fairy tale. Anything possible.
Stanley:	We're pleased to meet you, Mrs. Tarzan. I'm Stanley, he's Bottomley –
Bottomley:	Stanley, we've got no time for idle chatter! *(He spins around)*. They're coming closer! I can hear the pounding of their feet, the panting of their breath –
Stanley:	Shame, Bottomley – an Englishman should never forget his manners. Pardon me, Jane, but there's this dashed herd of elephants out yonder that's giving us quite a bit of bother. Nuisance really. Now, what can you do?
Jane:	*(looking off)* Me do what Tarzan teach Jane to do.
Bottomley:	What's that?
Jane:	Get the heck out of here!
Bottomley:	But how? We're surrounded!
Jane:	Me swing through trees giving Tarzan's bloodcurdling yell.
Stanley:	I've often wondered – why does he do that?
Jane:	Me don't know, but it sure scare the daylights out of jungle.
Bottomley:	Miss Jane, there aren't any trees here to swing through!
Jane:	Oh oh! Jane better call Tarzan.
Stanley:	That's the ticket! Imagine the great Tarzan, in the flesh.
Jane:	Not quite. Him wear loin cloth.
Bottomley:	Stanley, there's no time for this! Let's make a run for it!
Stanley:	Calm down, old chap – don't you get a kick out of meeting new people?
Bottomley:	Not when I'm about to be hammered six feet into the ground!
	(Jane has climbed up on the rock.)
Stanley:	Listen to this, Bottomley, the famous call of the jungle. See how she braces herself on that rock. See how she raises her cupped hands to her mouth. We're about to hear what no white man has ever heard –
Jane:	*(shouting)* Tarzan! Leave dishes and get lazy self over here, quick smart!

Bottomley: I've heard that before. It's why I came to the jungle.
(Jane climbs down off the rock. The distant sound of Tarzan's famous call is heard.)

Stanley: There it is, the real call of the jungle!
Jane: No, that Tarzan falling off roof. There are no trees over there either.

(Tarzan enters, limping and bruised. He, too, is dressed in skins and has a knife strapped to his waist.)

Tarzan: What happen to rotten trees? They there ten years ago.
Jane: Him not only clumsy, him not very bright. We in another part of the jungle ten years ago.
Tarzan: What you want, woman? Tarzan busy working on stamp collection.
Jane: Great white hunters in trouble.
Tarzan: Hullo, great white hunters. Me Tarzan, Lord of the Jungle! Me Tarzan the magnificent! Me Tarzan of the Apes!
Stanley: I don't see any apes.
Tarzan: Me just make that up when me saw you.
Bottomley: Humph! Off with you! An Englishman would rather be trampled than insulted.
Tarzan: Note Tarzan's beautiful body. Tarzan best swimmer in the world! Strongest man in the world! Fastest runner in the world! Second best wrestler in the world!
Stanley: Who's the best?
Tarzan: Jane. Tarzan a bit out of practice lately.
Jane: Tarzan live in a very small world. Him really King of the Chickens but him got big head.
Tarzan: They pretty fierce chickens, woman!
Bottomley: Stanley – the elephants!
Stanley: Oh, yes, Tarzan, be a good chap and do something spectacular to save us from the elephants.
Tarzan: What you after - cheap thrill? How you expect me to do that?
Bottomley: But you said you were the King of the Jungle.
Tarzan: You know that, me know that, chickens know that. But me have lots of trouble lately convincing elephants.
Jane: And Jane.
Bottomley: Can't you do anything?
Tarzan: Why not use magic-stick-that-speak-with-thunder-and-lightning?
Stanley: What magic stick, old boy?
Tarzan: That point-four-four calibre elephant gun with telescopic sights.
Stanley: Empty, I'm afraid. Dashed nuisance, really.
Tarzan: Then us in one big mess.
Jane: Him just work that out. Told you him not very bright.

Bottomley:	Can't you order them to go away? Don't you speak the language of all animals?
Tarzan:	What language elephant speak?
Stanley:	Better give it a try, Tarzan old thing. One good blast for the old school and all that.
Tarzan:	Me try.

(He climbs up on the rock and cups his hands around his mouth. The others look eagerly off.)

	Elephants, go home! *(There is a long pause.)*
Stanley:	They're not going.
Jane:	Still hope. Maybe they die laughing.
Tarzan:	Maybe they foreign elephants. We get many migrants this time of year.
Bottomley:	Do something! They're almost on us!
Jane:	Climb down, bigmouth. Jane try.

(Tarzan climbs down and Jane climbs up on the rock.)

Tarzan:	Ha! What can silly woman do that Tarzan can't do?
Jane:	*(shouting)* Elephants, go home or Jane come out there and give you good tongue lashing!

(There is a long pause.)

Stanley:	*(peering off)* They're going.
Bottomley:	Oh, man, look at them go.
Tarzan:	Beginner's luck.
Bottomley:	Incredible! We're saved! *(He laughs loudly.)*
Tarzan:	What wrong with him? Did Tarzan make joke?
Jane:	Tarzan one big joke. *(She climbs down.)*
Stanley:	I say, Jane, thanks a million. You saved our lives.
Jane:	Save Jane's life, too, but me do the same for you even if me not here.
Stanley:	However did you do it?
Jane:	What work on Tarzan work on elephants.
Tarzan:	No wonder me Tarzan of the Chickens.

Allan Mackay

TRAGEDY

JULIUS CAESAR

INTRODUCTION

Julius Caesar is a tragedy written by William Shakespeare. It follows the fortunes of Brutus, a good and honourable Roman. Julius Caesar, leader of the Roman Empire, has become very powerful. Many noblemen fear him and decide to kill him. They persuade Brutus to join them. He has no private reasons for murdering Caesar, but he believes it will be for the good of his country. His intentions are good. He is one of the group that stabs Caesar to death. This deed stains his nobility of character. Our respect for him weakens and he becomes a lesser man in our eyes. After the murder, the country is plunged into a war between those who supported Caesar and those who follow Brutus and his friends. Brutus had hoped to improve life for his fellow countrymen but his actions lead only to destruction and terror. In the final scene, Act V Scene V, his army is defeated and he knows the end is near.

SCENE V

(Another part of the field.)
Enter Brutus, Dardanius, Clitus, Strato, and Volumnius.

Brutus:	Come, poor remains of friends, rest on this rock.
Clitus:	Statilius show'd the torchlight, but, my lord,
	He came not back; he is or ta'en or slain.
Brutus:	Sit thee down, Clitus: slaying is the word;
	It is a deed in fashion. Hark thee, Clitus. *(Whispers.)*
Clitus:	What, I, my lord? No, not for all the world.
Brutus:	Peace then! No words.
Clitus:	I'll rather kill myself.
Brutus:	Hark thee, Dardanius. *(Whispers.)*
Dardanius:	Shall I do such a deed?
Clitus:	O Dardanius!
Dardanius:	O Clitus!
Clitus:	What ill request did Brutus make to thee?
Dardanius:	To kill him, Clitus. Look, he meditates.
Clitus:	Now is that noble vessel full of grief,
	That it runs over even at his eyes,

Brutus:	Come hither, good Volumnius; list a word.
Volumnius:	What says my lord?
Brutus:	Why, this, Volumnius:
	The ghost of Caesar hath appear'd to me
	Two several times by night; at Sardis once,
	And, this last night, here in Philippi fields;
	I know my hour is come
Volumnius:	Not so, my lord.
Brutus:	Nay, I am sure it is, Volumnius.
	Thou seest the world, Volumnius, how it goes;
	Our enemies have beat us to the pit: *(Low alarums.)*
	It is more worthy to leap in ourselves,
	Than tarry till they push us. Good Volumnius,
	Thou know'st that we two went to school together:
	Even for that our love of old, I prithee,
	Hold thou my sword-hilts, whilst I run on it.
Volumnius:	That's not an office for a friend, my lord. *(Alarum still.)*
Clitus:	Fly, fly, my lord; there is no tarrying here.
Brutus:	Farewell to you; and you; and you, Volumnius.
	Strato, thou hast been all this while asleep;
	Farewell to thee too, Strato. Countrymen,
	My heart doth joy that yet in all my life
	I found no man but he was true to me.
	I shall have glory by this losing day
	More than Octavius and Mark Antony
	By this vile conquest shall attain unto.
	So fare you well at once; for Brutus' tongue
	Hath almost ended his life's history:
	Night hangs upon mine eyes; my bones would rest,
	That have but labour'd to attain this hour.

(Alarum. Within 'Fly, fly, fly!')

Clitus:	Fly, my lord, fly.
Brutus:	Hence! I will follow.

(Exeunt Clitus, Dardanius, and Volumnius.)

	I prithee, Strato, stay thou by thy lord:
	Thou art a fellow of a good respect;
	Thy life hath had some snatch of honour in it:
	Hold then my sword, and turn away thy face,
	While I do run upon it. Wilt thou, Strato?
Strato:	Give me your hand first. Fare you well, my lord.
Brutus:	Farewell, good Strato. *(Runs on his sword.)*
	Caesar, now be still:
	I kill'd not thee with half so good a will.

(Dies. Alarum. Retreat. Enter Octavius, Antony, Messala, Lucilius, and the Army.)

Octavius:	What man is that?
Messala:	My master's man. Strato, where is thy master?
Strato:	Free from the bondage you are in, Messala;
	The conquerors can but make a fire of him;
	For Brutus only overcame himself,
	And no man else hath honour by his death.
Lucilius:	So Brutus should be found. I thank thee, Brutus,
	That thou hast proved Lucilius' saying true.
Octavius:	All that served Brutus, I will entertain them.
	Fellow, wilt thou bestow thy time with me?
Strato:	Ay, if Messala will prefer me to you.
Octavius:	Do so, good Messala.
Messala:	How died my master, Strato?
Strato:	I held the sword, and he did run on it.
Messala:	Octavius, then take him to follow thee,
	That did the latest service to my master.
Antony:	This was the noblest Roman of them all:
	All the conspirators save only he
	Did that they did in envy of great Caesar;
	He only, in a general honest thought
	And common good to all, made one of them.
	His life was gentle, and the elements
	So mix'd in him that Nature might stand up
	And say to all the world 'This was a man!'
Octavius:	According to his virtue let us use him,

> With all respect and rites of burial.
> Within my tent his bones tonight shall lie,
> Most like a soldier, order'd honourably.
> So call the field to rest, and let's away,
> To part the glories of this happy day. *(Exeunt.)*

William Shakespeare

EXPLORING THE TEXT

1 For whom is Brutus concerned?

2 What does he ask his friends to do for him?

3 What does he persuade Strato to do? Why?

4 His enemy, Antony, describes Brutus as 'the noblest Roman of them all.' Why does he say this?

5 How will his corpse be honoured?

6 What is your impression of Brutus, based on this scene?

7 Rewrite this scene as a piece of modern drama using modern English. Are the men soldiers or a street gang? What changes will you make to the costumes? Where will you locate the action – in a city, in a war-zone?

8 Choose one of the characters in either the original scene or in your updated version and perform the scene with the help of your classmates.

YOUR TURN

Write out a short play based on one of the short stories you have read. You are allowed to add to the dialogue if you wish.

Remember to:

• Write out the list of characters

• Describe the setting

 ▪ the scenery

 ▪ the costumes

 ▪ the props and the stage directions

MODERN DRAMA

ACROSS THE BARRICADES

INTRODUCTION

Across the Barricades is based on a novel by the same name, written by Joan Lingard. It is set in the late twentieth century in Northern Ireland. After an absence of three years, Kevin McCoy returns to Belfast, where he grew up, and meets Sadie Jackson. Kevin is a Catholic from a Nationalist background while Sadie is a Protestant from the Unionist tradition. They fall in love, but neither community is happy with their relationship. Soon they are forced to meet secretly, helped by Sadie's former teacher, Mr Blake.

Kevin is beaten up by Brian Rafferty because he refuses to fight the British and because he is dating Sadie, while Sadie comes under pressure from her family and friends to end her relationship with McCoy. The young couple face many difficulties together but tragedy strikes when Mr Blake's house is burnt down and he dies in the fire. Sadie suspects that he was attacked by members of her community, although Kevin fears that the attackers came from his own. Kevin realises that there is no hope for them and chooses to leave. Sadie must decide whether to stay in Belfast or to leave with him.

SCENE THREE

In Scene Three, Kevin and Sadie recall how they first met.

Cave Hill, evening. Sadie and Kevin enter and sit downstage.

Sadie:	It's beautiful up here, isn't it?
Kevin:	I love Cave Hill. I like sitting here, looking down on the city.
Sadie:	It looks so peaceful.
Kevin:	It does you good to get out of the city of an evening.
Sadie:	There's no one to bother you up here ...
Kevin:	Does it worry you about Linda seeing us?
Sadie:	It's none of her business.
Kevin:	Thought she was your best friend?
Sadie:	You're joking. Linda Mullet? She's just like her father, always out to cause trouble ... Don't know what our Tommy sees in her ...
Kevin:	So Tommy's going around with Linda?
Sadie:	She drags him all over Belfast and he pays.

Kevin:	Has he got a job then?
Sadie:	He works down there in the shipyards. What about you? Have you got a job?
Kevin:	Aye, remember Kate Kelly, you know, Brede's friend?
Sadie:	Yeah, what about her?
Kevin:	I'm working in her father's scrapyard.
Sadie:	Really? And does she go with the job?
Kevin:	Very funny!
Sadie:	She used to fancy you rotten, didn't she?
Kevin:	Hm, and what about you? What are you up to these days?
Sadie:	Trying to change the subject, are we? *(Laughing)* Must be some life roaming the streets looking for scrap.
Kevin:	Well, some of the scrap isn't exactly what you're looking for . . .
Sadie:	What about all these burnt out cars and things?
Kevin:	You daren't touch them. People use them . . . Burnt out cars, buses, torn-up paving stones, barbed wire . . . it might be scrap to you and me, but it comes in handy for building barricades . . . Oh, it's fun roaming the streets of Belfast . . . you see a bit of life . . .
Sadie:	Ah well, let's forget about all that.
Kevin:	Yeah, you're right.
	Pause. They look around, taking in the view.

Sadie:	It's funny seeing you after all this time.
Kevin:	And you . . .
Sadie:	I mean, after all, we only stay a few streets away from each other . . .
Kevin:	Yeah, but it might as well be a thousand miles.
Sadie:	Remember when we first met, when we were kids . . . we were sworn enemies.
Kevin:	It was a good laugh to begin with, a bit of a game right enough . . . Kevin's gang, Sadie's gang . . . calling each other names . . . *(Shouting)* Down with the Prods!
Sadie:	*(Shouting)* Down with the Micks!

As they begin to remember the past, it comes alive almost like a dream sequence.

Kevin:	I remember Brian and me sneaking into the Proddie's area in the middle of the night to paint over your lot's King Billy . . .
Sadie:	What about when I got into your house in the middle of the night and wrote 'Down with the Pope' on the kitchen table . . . it took poor Brede ages to scrape it off . . .
Kevin:	*(Almost to himself)* Oh, it started as a bit of fun all right . . .
Sadie:	*(Almost to herself, as if remembering a bad dream)* But it ended in a pitched battle . . . I remember as if it was yesterday . . . the eleventh of July . . . Bonfire Night . . . We were on one side of the road, they were on the other . . .

Music, sounds of the battle in full flight, children shouting, bin lids being bashed together, stone-throwing.

Kevin:	We'd been building up to it for days.
Sadie:	We started shouting 'Down with the Micks! Down with the Pope!'
Kevin:	*(Shouting)* Down with King Billy and all the Prods!

At this point, other members of the cast appear, playing the parts of other kids in the 'battle'. Together with Kevin and Sadie, they mime throwing stones and shout 'Down with the Prods' etc. as though the 'battle' is actually taking place. While this is going on, Sadie, Kevin, and other members of the cast narrate what happened, their voices charged with the excitement of the battle and almost having to shout above the noise.

Sadie:	People started throwing stones, then bricks . . .
Teenager 1:	Anything you could lay your hands on . . .
Teenager 2:	People were going mad . . .
Kevin:	Everyone was getting carried away with the excitement . . .
Sadie:	Everyone except Kevin's sister Brede . . . she just stood there, not shouting or throwing anything, just watching . . .

By now Brede has appeared in the middle of the battle, but she is not involved, she just stands very still.

Kevin:	Then someone threw a brick ... she tried to duck, but she wasn't quick enough ...
Sadie:	*(Screaming)* Brede!

Everyone freezes and for a few seconds there is silence, then other members of the cast walks off slowly, leaving Sadie and Kevin alone again.

Sadie:	Brede never hurt anyone ... in fact, the only time I'd ever met her she'd been very civil to me ... I ran to help her, it was just something I had to do ...
Kevin:	*(To Sadie)* I'll never forget that, you and Tommy helping Brede.
Sadie:	All I remember is waiting in that hospital, with you, me, and Tommy, wondering if Brede was going to die. Brede never harmed a soul and here she was the one that comes out worst when there's trouble.
Kevin:	After that we became friends. You, me, Tommy and Brede, when she recovered. We had some good times ... going off to the seaside at Bangor, coming up here ... we had a laugh ...
Sadie:	But it all got quite difficult, you know, telling our parents we were going somewhere else ... so we grew apart and that was that, until now ...
Kevin:	*(To Sadie)* We must do it again sometime ...
Sadie:	What?
Kevin:	Go to Bangor for the day, you and me like.
Sadie:	Well, when do you want to go?
Kevin:	How about Saturday?
Sadie:	We'll take a picnic, make a day of it, eh?
Kevin:	You're on!

Music. Sadie and Kevin exit.

EXPLORING THE TEXT

1 What do you learn about Sadie in this scene?

2 Give your impression of Kevin.

3 Why does Kevin worry about Linda Mullet?

4 Kevin and Sadie met in unusual circumstances. Do you agree? Explain your answer.

5 Describe the event that turned their hatred into friendship.

6 How important is the tone of voice in this scene? How does it affect the mood?

7 Comment on the use of sound effects in the scene.

8 What techniques does the playwright use to let the audience know that he has moved from the present to the past and back again?

9 Where is the climax of this scene?

10 Based on this scene alone, would you like to watch the play? Why or why not?

SCENE EIGHT

In Scene Eight, Kevin is threatened by Sadie's father and his friend, and by Brian Rafferty.

Near Sadie's street, 2 a.m.

Mr Jackson:	And what time of night is this to be wandering the streets?
Kevin:	I'm sorry if you've been worried about Sadie, Mr Jackson. We went to Bangor and missed the last bus . . .
Sadie:	And then we got a lift from Kevin's uncle and his car broke down . . .
Tommy:	I told you there would be a simple reason for it, Dad.
Mr Jackson:	Simple? That's not what I call it. We've been searching for hours looking for you . . .
Mr Mullet:	The whole street's been right upset and our Linda's nearly up the wall with worrying.
Sadie:	Well, she'll just need to get down again, won't she!
Mr Mullet:	The cheek of it . . .
Mr Jackson:	Your mother's in a terrible state. She'll be at the doctor's in the morning . . .
Sadie:	Aw, she's always at the doctor's . . .
Mr Jackson:	*(Going for her)* Why, you little . . .
Sadie:	*(Jumping clear)* All right, all right . . . I'm coming home now anyway, but I'm not going to be marched up the street as if I was being taken to jail.
Mr Mullet:	Jail would be too good for you. *(To Mr Jackson)* Sorry, Jim, but there's times a man must speak his mind. We've nearly been round the bend these last few hours thinking of all the things that might have happened to you.
Sadie:	Oh, did you think the Micks had got hold of me and tarred and feathered me?*
Kevin:	*(Under his breath)* Sadie!
Mr Mullet:	I wouldn't put anything past that lot.
Kevin:	Sadie, I'll be seeing you, OK?
Mr Jackson:	You just hold your horses, young fella, I'm not finished with you yet.
Tommy:	Oh, come on, let's go home to bed. We've found Sadie and that's

	the main thing.
Mr Jackson:	That's not the main thing at all. You two go home, I've got some unfinished business with this Mick.
Tommy:	Da, you're not going to start fighting.
Mr Jackson:	You don't seem to care who your sister's roaming around with till all hours of the night, but I do!
Sadie:	What do you want to fight Kevin for? He didn't force me to go with him ...
Kevin:	I don't want to fight anyone, Mr Jackson.
Mr Mullet:	No, 'cause you're probably too yellow! You lot are all the same!
Tommy:	For heaven's sake, let's go home.

Kevin grabs Mr Mullet by the collar. Mullet is taken off guard – he's not really too keen on doing the fighting himself.

Kevin:	Oh, you think we're yellow, do you? If you were my own age, I'd let you have it, but I don't pick on old men!
Mr Jackson:	Why you ...

He grabs Kevin, pushing Mullet out of the way.

	By the time I'm finished with you, you won't dare come near my daughter again ...
Sadie:	*(Pushing in between her father and Kevin)* If you want to fight Kevin, you'll have to take me on first!
Kevin:	I don't need you to fight my battles, Sadie.
Mr Jackson:	I'm going to break every bone in your body, McCoy!

Everyone is struggling. Tommy gets in between his father and Kevin and holds his father back.

Tommy:	*(Almost screaming)* Are you crazy? Break it up! If this goes on any longer, we'll have half the neighbourhood out on the streets. There's a mob gathering already up the road. We'll have a riot on our hands in a minute! Kevin, you'd best get out of here fast.
Sadie:	Tommy's right. Goodnight, Kevin. *(Panicking)* I said good night, Kevin!
Kevin:	OK, OK ... goodnight, Sadie, Tommy ...

He looks at Mr Jackson.

	Goodnight.

He walks away to the other side of the acting area.

Mr Jackson:	*(Shouting)* If I see you near my daughter again, I'll kill you!
Tommy:	*(Leading his father off)* All right, Da ... that's enough. Let's go.
Mr Mullet:	Tommy's right, Jim. Let's leave it for now.

Tommy leads his father away, Mr Jackson still shouting at Kevin. Mullet follows them. Just before they go off, they freeze: Mr Jackson is looking back at Kevin, threatening him, and Tommy is trying to restrain him. Kevin, now at the other side of the acting area, has his back to them. Sadie moves away from her father.

Sadie: *(To the audience)* I've never seen my father so angry. Through the anger and coldness in his face, I could see he was frightened. He wasn't frightened of Kevin, it was more what he represented. That night, my father became a stranger to me.

Mr Jackson, Tommy, and Mullet leave the stage, then Sadie follows them.

Kevin: *(To the audience)* I was lucky to get away before anyone else joined in. Sadie and I had arranged to meet up again the next day by the River Lagan, but after the little dust-up with her father I thought she might not want to risk it. My most immediate problem was trying to get home in one piece ...

Sound of an explosion, gunfire, shouting, etc. A soldier comes running on.

Soldier: *(Shouting)* Get down on the ground, son! You want to get killed?

Kevin: *(Obeying)* What in name's going on?

Soldier: Have you seen anyone running past you?

Kevin: I haven't seen anything.

Soldier: Aye, and if you had, you wouldn't be saying! *(Going)* You keep your head down for the next few minutes until you get an all clear ...

Kevin: Oh sure, anything you say!

The soldier runs off. Brian Rafferty creeps up behind Kevin and puts a finger to his neck as if it was a gun ...

Brian: It's all go tonight, eh Kevin?

Kevin: *(Turning around)* Brian! What are you doing creeping up on me like that?

Brian: *(Laughing)* You've missed all the action. Doyle's Bar got hit by the Prods. But don't worry, they're going to pay for this. They'd burn us out to the last man if we let them.

Kevin: We do a bit of burning ourselves.

Brian: I don't like the sound of that talk.

Kevin: What good does burning things do? I'm sick of fires.

Brian: So you take yourself off to Bangor for the day?

Kevin: How do you know that?

Brian: Your Uncle Albert's got a loose tongue. He told me all about your little trip to the seaside with your little blonde girl called Sadie.

Kevin: So what?

Brian: Think I'm daft? Only thing he didn't tell me, probably 'cause he didn't have the sense to know, was your little blonde girl was a Prod!

Kevin: It's none of your business.

Brian:	I remember Sadie all right, a fine little Loyalist!
Kevin:	You won't tell me what to do, Rafferty, so don't even think of it.
Brian:	No? Oh, well, we'll see . . . *(Laughing)* Take care going home, Kevin, these are dangerous times!

Brian goes off quickly. Music.

*Tarring and feathering involves smearing a person with tar and then covering him/her with feathers. it was used by Republicans as a method of 'punishing' or frightening people.

EXPLORING THE TEXT

1 What worries Mr Jackson more – the fact that his daughter is out so late or the fact that she is with Kevin? Give reasons for you answer.
2 How does the playwright deal with the theme of conflict here?
3 Who is the peacemaker? Is he successful?
4 'Take care going home, Kevin, these are dangerous times.' What do you think Brian means? How would you direct an actor to speak these words?
5 What piece of music would you choose to use at the end of this scene? Explain your choice.

SCENE TWENTY

In the final scene Kevin has made up his mind to leave Belfast. He is taking the boat to England.

Belfast docks, midday. Kevin is standing by Sadie, holding his suitcase.

Kevin:	I've had enough, Sadie. I never thought I'd see the day when I'd want to leave Belfast . . . But I'm sick of it all . . . sick of all the killings. I keep wondering who put that bomb through Mr Blake's window. Was it one of my so-called friends? Would Brian Rafferty really go that far?
Sadie:	It could have been someone I know, someone from my street.
Kevin:	What sort of place has this become? I'd like to walk down a street where there were no soldiers with guns, no policemen with their fingers on triggers . . . and no bloody graffiti on the walls . . . there must be more to life than all of that . . .

Sadie: My mother was shouting at me again yesterday. Everything's back to normal. It's nearly a week now since they buried Mr Blake . . . 'Well, Sadie, you've learned your lesson now' . . . that's what she said, no kiddin', and she meant it. My father is convinced it was one of your lot . . . I told him just to go to hell. I said it could just as easily have been him next door, your good friend Mr Mullet . . . I thought he was going to hit me . . . he stood up and came over to me and looked me in the eye . . . but before he could say anything, I started crying, I felt I was going to burst . . . so he didn't hit me, he put his arms around me and held me. That was worse – he was trying to comfort me and I just felt cold all through my body . . . I wish to God he had hit me, it would have made it easier!

Kevin: Parents! My mother thinks I should have taken back my old job at Kelly's. She doesn't want to face up to things . . . I can understand it in a way, they've got to go on living in that street. Brede was all right though, she helped me to pack . . . she understands, she knows . . . I'll miss Brede, you know, I really will . . . I'll miss Belfast . . . *(Laughing)* I'm feeling homesick already and I'm not even on the ferry . . .

Sadie: Did you think I wouldn't come?

Kevin: I knew you'd be here . . . the trouble is, I don't want to say goodbye to you . . .

Sadie: Kevin, I haven't come to say goodbye . . .

Kevin: *(Laughing nervously)* No, of course, we'll see each other again.

Sadie: You don't understand, do you? Look, I've bought a ticket. I'm coming with you. That is, if you don't mind?

Kevin: Sadie, are you kidding?

Sadie: *(Excited)* I've no luggage. I couldn't walk out of the house with a case, so you'll have to take me as I stand.

| Kevin: | Sadie, this is the best news I've had in months. |

He picks her up and swings her round. They kiss.

| Sadie: | (Smiling) Come on then, let's get aboard. What are we waiting for? |
| Kevin: | Nothing. London here we come! |

Kevin picks up his case and they turn to go, but freeze. We hear their voices on tape again, with music in the background.

Sadie:	(Off) And that was just the beginning . . .
Kevin:	(Off) You should have seen Sadie on the boat. I've never seen anyone looking so ill in all my life, honestly . . .
Sadie:	(Laughing) Sshhh . . . shut up, Kevin . . . you're not meant to tell them about that . . .

We hear them both laughing, then the laughter fades.

| Newsreader: | (Off) Capital Radio, newsflash. A bomb has exploded in the centre of London today. It is understood that the explosion was caused by a car bomb. Unconfirmed reports say that at least five people have been killed and over a hundred have been injured. No one has claimed responsibility for the incident but a police spokesman confirmed that eight people have been detained under the Prevention of Terrorism Act. An emergency telephone number has been given for relatives and friends. The number is 01-779 . . . (fade). |

As the newsflash fades, the music comes up.

During the newsflash, Sadie and Kevin turn back to face the audience. The other members of the cast come back onto the stage. They all stand motionless as they hear the news report.

After the newsflash, the music builds, then fades.

Extract from *Across the Barricades* by Joan Lingard adapted by Ian Neville (Oxford Playscripts, 2003), copyright © David Neville 1990, reprinted by permission of Oxford University Press.

EXPLORING THE TEXT

1   What drives Kevin away?

2   Why does Sadie decide to leave also?

3   What is the significance of the final news bulletin?

4   Do you feel that this is a satisfactory ending to the play? Why or why not?

5   How would you describe the play – as a comedy, a tragedy or a tragi-comedy? Explain your answer.

YOUR TURN

- **Write a short scene showing what happens when Kevin and Sadie reach London.**
- **Write a scene between any two of the characters who are looking back thirty years later at the events that occurred in the play.**
- **Choose one of the scenes above and perform it with your friends. Notice how other groups in your class performed the same scene.**
- **Write a short play, or a scene from a play, about two people from different backgrounds who meet – you can choose from one of the following if you like:**
  - **a rich girl and a poor young man**
  - **a Palestinian Muslim and an Israeli Jew**
  - **an American soldier and an Iraqi woman**

Taking part in a drama production can be a great experience. Even if you do not like acting there is always a need for someone to:

- Direct
- Prompt
- Design costumes
- Make props
- Design scenery
- Take charge of sound, lighting and special effects
- Take charge of the curtain

- Audition
- Help at rehearsals
- Help with make-up
- Arrange the seating
- Advertise
- Sell tickets
- Do all the important odd jobs!

So why not have some fun? Join a drama group or begin one in your school, with some help from your friends and the Principal's permission.

CHAPTER 12

NEWSPAPERS AND CARTOONS

WHAT YOU WILL LEARN IN THIS CHAPTER

- The importance of newspapers
- To identify broadsheets and tabloids
- The layout and structure of newspapers, news reports, editorials and letters to the editor
- The structure of cartoons

HOW YOU WILL LEARN

- Creating your own media folder
- Reading news reports, letters, editorials and cartoons
- Studying the layout of newspapers and cartoons
- Analysing reports and cartoons
- Producing your own newspaper
- Drawing your own cartoons

INTRODUCING NEWSPAPERS

Newspaper publishing is a major industry. Every day over half a million newspapers are sold in Ireland. There are three types of newspaper – local, national and foreign or imported papers.

Irish newspapers print local, national and international news. They comment on Irish affairs from an Irish perspective. They also provide hundreds of jobs in areas such as production, sales, distribution, advertising and marketing.

Some newspapers sold in Ireland are Irish editions of UK newspapers. They may employ a team of Irish based journalists to cover the Irish news and sport, but the bulk of the newspaper is identical to that produced for the UK market. These newspapers can be sold more cheaply than newspapers which are completely produced in Ireland. The share of the market captured by these newspapers is growing.

EXPLORING THE TEXT

1 How important is the newspaper industry in Ireland?
2 What might influence a person in their choice of newspaper?
3 Is it important that Irish national and local news are covered in the newspapers we read? Explain your answer.

FUNCTIONS OF A NEWSPAPER

The aim of a newspaper is to sell as many copies as possible. A newspaper must fulfil a number of functions in order to do this. These functions are:

- To inform readers of recent newsworthy events
- To report those events accurately
- To expose dishonest or criminal activities by individuals, an organisation or a group. Newspapers are said to act as **watchdogs** to protect the public interest
- To explain and analyse the news and offer opinions on its significance
- To give readers an opportunity to express their opinions on the letter page
- To entertain readers with light-hearted articles, games and crosswords
- To inform readers about social and cultural events
- To review cultural material
- To advertise products, services and events

THE STAFF

The Editor

The editor has overall responsibility for the newspaper. He or she decides on the content of the paper.

Sub-editors

Sub-editors check and correct material sent in for publication and draw up the plans for the layout of each page. Headlines are written to draw attention to the article.

Other editors

News, business and sports editors are responsible for their own departments. They have their own staff of reporters, correspondents and sub-editors.

Picture editors

Picture editors work on the picture desk. They use staff photographers, freelance photographers and picture agencies to supply the paper's pictures.

Features editors

Feature editors have separate staff providing human interest pieces, articles on the arts and entertainment and lifestyle pieces, e.g. gardening, motoring and travel.

Graphics dept.	Graphic artists produces logos, diagrams, charts, maps and artwork for all the departments.
Distribution	This department ensures that the paper is collected from the printers and delivered to shops nationwide.

SOURCES

Reporters	Every newspaper employs reporters to investigate and write news stories. Some will concentrate on specific areas such as the courts, foreign affairs, finance and politics.
News agencies	News agencies gather news from around the world and sell it to newspapers. Reuters, an international news agency, is one of the best known.
Stringers	Newspapers do not have reporters in every country. Stringers are journalists who are contacted by a newspaper to report on an event in their own country.

Press conferences	Press conferences are held to release information to a large number of journalists at the same time. Usually they are held by organisations, although important individuals may hold press conferences also.
Press releases	Press releases are articles sent to newspapers by individuals and groups who wish to make an announcement to the public.
Leaks	Confidential information may be 'leaked' in secret to a journalist. The information may embarrass an organisation or an individual, or may alert the press to some dishonest activity taking place. The person who gives the journalist the information is not identified.

BROADSHEETS AND TABLOIDS

Newspapers have two basic formats – the tabloid and the broadsheet. The broadsheet is a sheet of paper the full size of a rotary press plate, an A2 page. The tabloid is half the size of a broadsheet. It is printed on an A3 page. The term 'tabloid' can be used to describe a simplistic, sensationalistic style of journalism. It may also refer to the layout of the stories on the page.

'Middle-of-the-road' newspapers lie between 'quality' broadsheet newspapers and 'popular' tabloids.

In general, broadsheet newspapers provide detailed, accurate, factual reporting in a balanced, neutral manner. They concentrate on serious news items and rarely use sensational, dramatic or emotive language.

Tabloids focus on popular culture, dramatic news stories, sports and celebrity gossip. They are less concerned with wider issues such as the economy, politics, foreign affairs or serious news items. They often use emotive language. Emotive language plays upon the emotions of the reader. Words such as 'yobs', 'thugs', and 'fanatical' create images in the reader's mind. The tabloids use of sensational and emotive language means their reports can be biased in favour of or against certain organisations, beliefs, nationalities or individuals. This bias will reflect and reinforce the bias of their readers.

It is important to remember, however, that not all tabloid reports are trivial and biased and not all broadsheet stories are balanced and informative.

YOUR TURN

Name one example of each of the following:

- **A national broadsheet (morning)**
- **A national tabloid (evening)**
- **A local newspaper**
- **A foreign broadsheet**
- **A foreign tabloid**

FEATURES OF NEWSPAPERS

TABLOIDS

LANGUAGE

(Purpose: to attract interest and hold attention)

Dramatic

Vivid

Descriptive

Informal

Personal

Emotive

Biased

Conversational: uses slang, clichés, idioms

(idiom: an expression used in everyday speech)

STORIES/ARTICLES

Focus on human interest aspects of event

Little information

Frequent use of quotations

Opinions given

PHOTOGRAPHS

Extensive use of photographs

Many colour photographs

May invade privacy of individual

PRINT SIZE

Variety of print sizes used to make story appear more interesting

Capital letters, standard format, bold print and italics may appear in the same article

HEADLINES

Heavy, eye-catching headlines

Usually short

May be provocative

CONTENT

Dramatic, sensational news

Stories focus on popular culture, television, film and the music world

BROADSHEETS

LANGUAGE

(Purpose: to inform)

Factual

Clear

Economical

Formal

Neutral

Detached

Balanced

STORIES/ARTICLES

Focus on events of national or international importance

Detailed information

Few quotations

Neutral approach

PHOTOGRAPHS

Some photographs used

Some colour photographs

PRINT SIZE

Generally small

HEADLINES

Bold print

Often long

Indicates content of report/article

CONTENT

Important, well-researched news

Stories focus on the economy, politics and global issues

ANALYSING NEWSPAPERS

Study the key terms below to help you analyse newspapers.

Masthead	The masthead is the name of a newspaper. It appears on top of the front page. The mastheads of tabloids are usually red or white, while broadsheets usually use black print.
Banner headline	The banner headline is the main headline.
Headline	The headline indicates the content of the article.
Sub-headings	Sub-headings provide more information about the article.
Byline	The byline tells the reader the name of the journalist who wrote the piece.
Caption	The caption gives information on a photograph.
Columns	Newspaper articles are printed in rows called columns.
Filler	A filler is a short, interesting news item used to fill space on a page.
Features	Features include background articles, human interest pieces, articles on the arts, entertainment and lifestyle areas.

LAYOUT

The front page is designed to attract attention, arouse curiosity and persuade people to buy the newspaper.

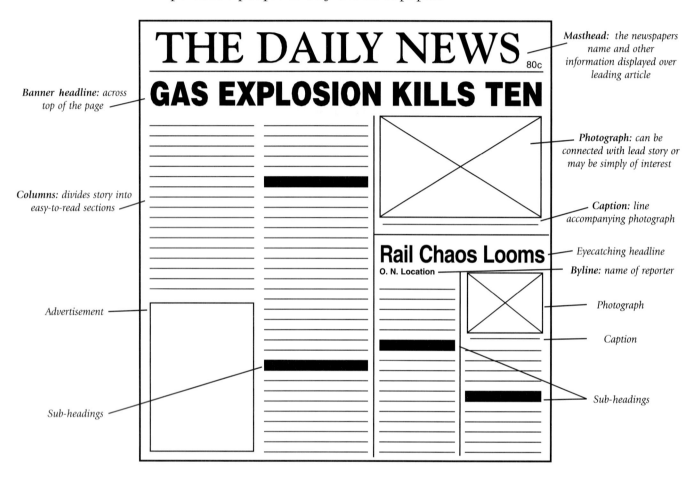

The differences between the broadsheet and the tabloid are clearly seen in the layout of their front pages. The broadsheet will usually print a number of stories, use small print, and provide one colour photograph and perhaps one advertisement on the front page. The headlines are factual and indicate the content of the accompanying stories. They are rarely sensational.

The tabloid front page is normally colourful, with a large eye-catching headline and colour photograph, a single story, very little text and a variety of print sizes.

TYPOGRAPHY

Printers use a variety of typefaces to make the newspaper look more interesting.

THE DAILY NEWS

LARGE PRINT — Bold print to attract attention

EYE-CATCHING! — Reverse headline (white on black)

DIFFERENT size of print
make reading an
article more interesting

HEADLINES

Headlines play an important role in attracting the readers' attention, arousing their curiosity and providing information on the nature of the article.

They are usually:
• Short
• Descriptive
• Dramatic or sensational

A form of shorthand is often used to reduce the amount of space they require. For example, 'The Head of the Tourism Board Resigns' may be reduced to 'Tourism Chief Quits'.

Some words are repeated in headlines. 'Chaos', 'Fear', 'Horror', 'Slam', 'Scare' 'Furious', 'Shock' and 'Rage' appear very frequently.

Puns

A pun is a clever or witty play upon a word. They are never used in serious reports or when writing about tragedies, but may be used for less important stories and in sports reports. 'Snow Joke' or 'Owen Goal' are typical examples of puns in headlines.

Clichés

Clichés are phrases that are over used, such as 'a window of opportunity'. Tabloids use clichés, or variations on them, more often than the broadsheets.

Alliteration

Alliteration is used to catch the reader's attention, e.g. 'Lucky Limerick Lady Scoops Lotto' or 'Cork Chess Champ Claims Cup'.

Rhyme

Rhyme is also used to arouse the reader's interest, e.g. 'Dumb Mum Forgets Son' is a headline for a story about a mother who left her baby son in a supermarket.

YOUR TURN

- Create your own media folder. Collect three different newspapers – a broadsheet, a tabloid and a 'middle-of-the-road' paper and keep them in the folder.
- Make a list of the contents of the papers and note the number of pages given to each type of article in the different papers. How many sports pages are there? How many pages given over to politics, to celebrity gossip, to national events and so on?

- Examine the headlines in the different newspapers and make out a list of the ten most commonly used words.
- Using some of the techniques above, make up your own headlines for articles on:
  - a fire at a factory
  - the discovery of a treasure trove
  - the sale of a famous painting
  - a victory by a sports team
  - a heavy snow storm
  - the failure of a famous person to turn up at a major event

WRITING THE NEWS

Newspaper articles answer the questions: Who? What? Where? When? Why? How?

WHO?

These are the people involved in the event. Famous people, politicians, singers and stars make a story more newsworthy.

WHAT?

What happens must be important and/or of interest to the readers. Tabloid and broadsheet editors take their readers into account when deciding if the story will or will not be printed.

WHERE?

Where the event occurs can determine whether or not it appears in the paper. A taxi strike in Outer Mongolia may not appear in an Irish paper – a taxi strike in Dublin will!

WHEN?

Old news is no news, it's history. Newspapers concentrate on events that are recent, usually something that has happened in the previous twenty-four hours. Pressure from television, radio and other forms of mass media means that papers have to be up to date or they will not sell.

WHY?

The reason for the occurrence must be given and explained.

HOW?

Articles usually describe how the action took place and how people were affected.

THE OPENING SENTENCE

The opening sentence of a report attempts to answer all of these questions at once! The rest of the story gives more information. Opinions and quotes are left to the end. This is sometimes referred to as an inverted pyramid.

SUMMARY STATEMENT
IMPORTANT INFORMATION
OTHER INFORMATION
OPINIONS
QUOTES

If there is pressure for space the opinions and quotes can be edited out without changing the main body of the report.

Here is a report about a disaster at sea. You can see how the opening sentence is structured. If you wish to find out more information you must read the whole report.

Who? The crew of the trawler 'The Maryann'
What? was rescued
How? by local fishermen
Where? from the sea near the Blasket Islands
When? on Saturday night
Why? When their boat sank during high winds.

The crew of the trawler 'The Maryann' was rescued from the sea near the Blasket Islands by local fishermen on Saturday night when their boat was capsized by a freak wave during a heavy storm.

'The Maryann' was returning to port when the ten metre high wave struck, causing the trawler to keel over. The vessel took in water and sank within minutes. The crew survived by clinging to plastic crates that floated from the hold to the surface.

'We are lucky to be alive,' said Sonny Molloy, the relieved captain of 'The Maryann'. 'Fortunately we had time to send out a may-day with our position before she went down.' The fact that all three men on board were wearing life-jackets is also believed to be a contributory factor in their survival.

1 Give this report a headline and a byline.

2 Edit the report to approximately one-third its length without losing any important information.

3 Find a report in one of the papers in your media folder and identify the opening statement. Based on your reading of the report, answer the questions who, what, why, when, where and how?

4 Write your own report on a disaster (an airplane crash, a car accident, a major earthquake etc.) for either a tabloid or a broadsheet newspaper and add it to your file.

YOUR TURN

• **Read the following articles and then complete the exercises below.**

ARTICLE I

At last eggs have been given a clean bill of health. American nutritionist Donald McNamara says an egg a day will not increase the risk of heart disease. Since 1968 people with high cholesterol levels have been advised to reduce their egg intake. Dr McNamara revealed that a study by Harvard School of Public Health of 117,000 men and women could find no link between eating eggs and heart disease.

ARTICLE 2

Food expert Dr Donald McNamara yesterday dismissed claims that eggs are bad for you. 'Eggs are far healthier than a fatty cut of red meat,' he said. Dr McNamara, executive director of Washington DC's Egg Nutrition Centre, studied 117,000 men and women in America. He said 'For most there is no risk. An egg a day is fine.'

Newspapers not only report the news, they also analyse and comment on newsworthy events. Editorials provide interesting reading. They may offer advice, make general observations, praise or criticise sections of society or actions taken by various bodies, including the government.

Read the following editorial and then find one in a newspaper, cut it out and place it in your media folder.

EDITORIALS

In overall terms the government will be pleased by the performance of the economy. Despite the threat of inflation prospects are good. Exchequer returns are rising and there is an increase in the number of people gainfully employed.

The only cloud on the horizon is the rise in the number of young people leaving school without qualifications. This is due to the present demand for unskilled workers. Many students, especially young men, are being lured from the classroom by what seems to be good wages. There is a current need for unskilled labourers on building sites and construction projects throughout the country and young people are tempted by what appears to be easy money. Unfortunately what may be a good salary at sixteen is not adequate at twenty-six. Young people living at home have few expenses. Adults with families to support and other financial responsibilities cannot survive on a similar wage. Yet workers without even basic qualifications will not be in a position to demand higher wages in the future. When the economic boom is over they will be the first to lose their jobs. Their chances of finding new employment will be very slim. This is a clear case of the short-term gain being a long-term loss.

School principals and career guidance teachers should make every effort to encourage their pupils to remain within the education system. The ultimate responsibility however lies with the parents to ensure that their children remain in school, until they have their Junior Certificate at least.

●●●●● EXPLORING THE TEXT ●●●●

1 Why should the government be pleased?
2 What is the only problem at present, according to the editorial?
3 Why are young people leaving school early?
4 What work related problems will they experience later in life?
5 According to the editorial, who has the greatest responsibility to ensure that students remain in school?
6 Find the editorials in your newspapers. Compare them in terms of content, style and length.

The letters' section of the newspaper gives the readers an opportunity to respond to some of the articles that were printed, to comment on current affairs and to express their concerns about or interest in topical issues.

Due to pressure of space in newspapers, the letters have the following layout:

Sir,–

I was horrified to read that Japan has ruined plans for a new whale sanctuary in the South Pacific. The new sanctuary would have provided a safe home for the humpback whale, whose numbers have slumped from 100,000 to 15,000. Conservationists now fear the Japanese intend a new slaughter of these gentle creatures. This butchery must be stopped before the whale becomes extinct.

Yours, etc.,

Frank Fahy

Mayfield,

Cork.

Sir,–

As a teenage girl, I would like to express my concern about the portrayal of women in teen magazines and by the media generally. Desirable, fashionable women are almost always shown to be unnaturally slim. Nearly all successful models are under weight. This leads to the dangerous belief that thin is beautiful. Now girls as young as ten are dieting to gain the 'ideal' shape. This in turn leads to serious health problems in their teenage years. I think editors of these magazine have a responsibility to their readers to depict women as they really are and not as some fashion designer thinks they should be.

Yours, etc.,

Eileen Hurley

Mullingar,

Co. Westmeath.

Madam,–

Why are Irish people incapable of putting litter in a bin or simply taking it home? While out walking on a beach last Sunday I found myself wading though piles of rubbish left by day-trippers. Tin cans, bottles, crisp bags, cigarette packets, soiled nappies, plastic bags, foam packaging and discarded suntan lotion bottles were strewn along the sand. The litter bin itself was only half full. This is a sad reflection on our attitude towards the environment and our lack of consideration for others who will visit the beach after we are gone.

Surely we can do better than this?

Yours, etc.,

Moira Greene

Terenure,

Dublin 6.

Sir,–

Congratulations on your brilliant coverage of recent major sports events. 'The Daily News' provided really excellent reports and analysis of the soccer and GAA finals. Though not a great sports fan I enjoyed reading these informative articles every day.

Yours, etc.,

John Power

Waterford.

YOUR TURN

- **Write a letter to the editor on a topic or issue you feel strongly about and put it in your media folder.**
- **Create your own front page for a newspaper (tabloid or broadsheet) and add it to the folder. Remember to include:**
- **the masthead**
- **banner headline**

- columns
- photographs (or drawings)
- captions
- bylines
- headlines
- sub-headings
- reports in the appropriate style

- Produce a class newspaper. Choose your staff. You will need:
  - an editor
  - a sub-editor
  - journalists
  - a student who will design the masthead, the banner headline and sub-headings, and advertisements
  - printers

- Now your staff is in place you must decide on the type newspaper - a broadsheet, middle-of-the-road or tabloid:
  - the name of the newspaper
  - the lead story
  - other stories (features, human interest, lifestyle etc.)
  - the editorial
  - reviews
  - crosswords, horoscopes etc.
  - each student should send a letter to the editor. A selection of letters will be printed

Ask for permission to photocopy your newspaper and distribute it to your classmates.

INTRODUCING COMIC STRIPS

Comic strips are narratives. They tell stories in pictures and words. They have an introduction, a complication and a resolution. Comic strips are sometimes called cartoons. The word 'cartoon' originally referred to an artist's sketch drawn on paper, not on canvas. A cartoon story can be found in comic books and a strip cartoon in a newspaper. Some advertisements use cartoons to attract our attention.

FEATURES OF HUMOROUS CARTOONS

Characters Cartoon characters are well-known types, e.g. a burglar, a scruffy schoolboy, a wealthy lady.

Setting Cartoons are set in recognisable locations, e.g. the classroom, the office, a city street.

Plot Every cartoon tells a story. There is a clear beginning, middle and end.

Conflict Many cartoons deal with a fight or disagreement between the characters. Usually the conflict is between the bully and the schoolboy, the teacher and the student, the parent and the child.

Action Most cartoons show something exciting happening to the main character.

Humour Cartoons use humour to make their point.

- The cartoon is sketched in boxes called frames or panels.
- The location or background is drawn using very little detail. A computer and a desk sets the scene in an office; a barred window suggests a jail; a skyscraper tells you that the action is taking place in a city.
- Shading creates the effect of light and shadows and suggests the mood of the piece.
- The faces and bodies of the characters are exaggerated. The hero has a strong jaw line and bulging muscles. The heroine is beautiful. The villain is sly and evil.

TECHNIQUES

- Gestures, facial expressions and other forms of body language tell you how the character feels.
- Speech balloons contain direct speech. The balloon tail points to the speaker. As space in a cartoon is limited, very few words are used. Print size tells you how loudly the characters are speaking. They whisper in small print, shout in **BOLD TYPE**, and stress their words in *italics*. Question marks may indicate surprise and puzzlement, while exclamation marks make the statement more dramatic!!!
- Thought bubbles allow us to 'see' what a character is thinking.
- Action is suggested by using double lines, splashes, sweat marks, stars and gestures.
- Changes in time may be indicated in the upper portion of the panel. 'Then' and 'later' are used most often.

Read the comic strip below to see how the artist used these techniques to tell a story.

'For Better or For Worse' is a popular comic strip by Lynn Johnston.

1 Where is the action taking place?
2 Why is Michael slumped over his homework in the fourth and fifth frames?
3 Give your opinion of his mother's advice.
4 What surprise awaits the reader in the last frame?
5 What is the cartoonist's purpose in creating this comic strip? Is it to entertain, to inform, to educate or to make us think?

- Cut a cartoon from a comic book or a newspaper and paste it into your copy.
  - Jot down the number of frames used by the artist.
  - Mark in your copy the techniques used to tell the story.
  - What is the purpose of the cartoon?
  - Write out the names of the characters.
  - Do the names tell you something about their personalities?
  - Write out the plot in your own words. Is there conflict in the story? If so, what type of conflict is it?
- Draw your own cartoon. Give it a title and see how many of the techniques above you can use to make it interesting.

CHAPTER 13

ADVERTISING

WHAT YOU WILL LEARN IN THIS CHAPTER

- How advertisements are designed
- The aim of advertising
- What techniques are used to persuade the consumer

HOW YOU WILL LEARN

- Reading examples of advertising
- Responding to different advertisements
- Creating your own advertisements

INTRODUCING ADVERTISING

We are constantly bombarded by advertising – in newspapers and magazines, on radio, television and the Internet, on posters and buses, even in the cinema.

The aims of advertising are:

- To inform the public about goods and services
- To persuade people to buy something or to behave in a certain way
- To launch a new product or service
- To announce a change in a product
- To make a brand name familiar
- To make the consumer aware that choices exist
- To convince the consumer of the quality of the good or service so that he or she will buy it
- To buy the product again

An advertiser knows that he or she must get our attention, impress the name of the product or service on us, and persuade us that we need that product or service to enjoy happy, healthy and fulfilled lives.

Advertisements play on our desires and weaknesses in order to persuade us that this product will solve all our problems. To make us buy they:

- Create an image we find attractive, e.g. the successful business man, the good mother, the successful career woman, the caring father or the popular teenager
- Promise improvements, e.g. reverse aging, give us white teeth, make us desirable, make us thin, make us fit and healthy
- Suggest that our lives will be better if we use the product or service
- Promise a bargain

Nearly all advertisement use some of the following:

- Buzz words, e.g. *new, improved, fresh, stronger, longer lasting, extra, care*
- Repetition – especially the name of the good or service to make it easier to remember

- Colour to create a feeling, e.g. green is fresh, blue is cool and orange is warm
- Unusual spelling to attract our attention, e.g. 'Beanz Meanz Heinz'
- Humour
- Well-known personalities who endorse the product or service
- Questions to make us curious and read the advertisement
- Special offers or free samples or coupons to tempt us
- Scientific jargon to impress or appear to support the claims being made
- Well-known sayings, proverbs and catchphrases
- Illustrations

THE TARGET AUDIENCE

Advertisements are aimed at specific groups known as the **target audience** – the main market for the good or service. They are designed to appeal to that audience. Most mobile telephones are sold to young people and people in the business community, therefore few of these advertisements feature people over the age of fifty. Teenagers and young single wage earners are the target of many advertisements, as manufacturers know that these people have disposable incomes and are not yet burdened by mortgages and other financial commitments.

IMPORTANT TERMS

Study the key words below which will help you to analyse an advertisement.

Brand name	The make of the product.
Caption	The text related to the picture.
The composition	The way objects are arranged in the picture.
Copy	The text of the advertisement (not the headlines).
Upper case	Capital letters.
Lower case	Small letters.
Logo	The name of the company with its trademark symbol.
Slogan	A memorable, catchphrase related to the product, the service or the provider.

Typography	The print used in the text.
Visuals	The photograph, illustration or logo used in the advertisement.
Coupon	A part of the advertisement that is intended to be cut out, filled in and returned to the company.

Advertisements sell their products by sending out messages on the conscious level and also on the subconscious level. These are known as the overt message and the covert message.

On a conscious level we are aware of the product and the printed text, if any.

On a subconscious level we are influenced by the use of:

• Colour
• Props
• Lighting and
• The message contained within the printed text.

COLOUR

Advertisers are aware that humans respond to different colours in different ways. Colours have certain associations for us:

Green: Refreshing, natural, quiet

Yellow: Cheerful, energetic

Orange: Lively, strong

Red: Exciting, active, warm, dangerous

White: Clean, young, pure

Black: Depressing, evil, threatening

Purple: Rich, dignified

Blue: Clean, fresh, cold

BODY LANGUAGE

We respond to the gestures and expressions of people and animals. A person engaged in an enjoyable activity creates a sense of energy and wellbeing, whereas someone slouched in an old armchair has a draining effect.

We also read facial expression very well. A smiling person generates a positive response in us while a frowning face has the opposite effect.

LIGHTING

Lighting can influence our way of looking at a product. Harsh lighting makes everything seem cold. Soft, warm lighting make things seem more attractive. Shadows may suggest gloom, something threatening or something mysterious.

PROPS

Props are always carefully chosen by advertisers. They add to our image of the product. A box of chocolates may be placed by an expensive crystal glass. This suggests that a certain class of person eats these chocolates. If the chocolates were placed beside an overflowing dustbin the advertisement would send out a very different message!

TEXT

The text is carefully written to appeal to the consumer. Words such as 'smooth', 'luxury', 'hygienic' and 'healthy' evoke clear responses in the reader. On a subconscious level the text may flatter or frighten us, encouraging us to use the product or behave in the way suggested by the advertisement.

ANALYSING AN ADVERTISEMENT

Use the questions on pages 302 and 303 to analyse the Domestos advertisement.

Hygiene to Go

Clare McKeon has always worked to a full schedule, recently adding the "Bliss" beauty salon to her media career. But Neil is part of the daily agenda too. He needs just the same care and attention as any other toddler.

So Clare is delighted with Domestos Wipes. They provide the confidence of hygenic cleaning in a convenient wipe format. She finds that carrying a box around leaves her prepared for any little emergencies.

Domestos Wipes -
instant hygiene for busy people.

We're here to help!

Domestos

HYGIENE ADVISORY SERVICE
Freephone RoI 1850 301 302
www.hygienexpert.com

HYGIENE TO GO

Product name

1. What product is being advertised?
2. How many times does the brand name appear?
3. Why is the name repeated so often?
4. What logo is used?
5. Where does it appear?

Illustration

1. Briefly describe the scene.
2. What props are used?
3. Why did the advertiser decide to use fruit and vegetables?
4. What does this suggest about the mother?
5. What do you notice about the surface of the table and the steel fittings in the kitchen? How are they linked with the product?
6. Why did the advertiser decide to locate the advertisement in a kitchen?

Colour

1. Why did the advertiser choose red-browns and reds in the background?
2. What colours do the manufacturers use on the Domestos box?
3. What do these colours suggest?
4. What colour is the tissue? Why is it not black?
5. Why is the colour green included?

Facial expression

1. Describe the facial expressions of the two people in the illustration.
2. Why were they told to pose in this way?
3. What connection is there between their expressions and the product?
4. How does the consumer respond to their expressions?
5. Based on your reading of the image, what kind of mother is Clare McKeon?

Product

1. Why are we given three shots of the product?
2. What buzz word appears on the box?
3. Where is the product used?
4. What claim is made for the wipes?
5. How many wipes are in each box?

Text

1. Do you think the caption is good? Explain your answer.
2. What claims are made for the product?
3. Who is the target audience?
4. Is the price mentioned?
5. Are there any technical or scientific terms used? Why?
6. Does the advertisement use words or phrases that evoke pleasant feelings?
7. What image of the company do the advertisers wish to promote?
8. Is there any reference to experts? In what context? Why is the information included in the advertisement?
9. Why did the advertisers use Clare McKeon to promote this product?
10. In your opinion, is this a successful advertisement?

Study the Seat advertisment on page 304, and answer the questions which follow.

For those who believe in driving.

Dynamic Steering Response (DSR) ensures the new SEAT Leon reacts instantly and precisely to the ever-changing demands of the road. With five outstanding engines to choose from, led by the 2.0 TFSI 185PS and the 2.0 TDI 140PS, the new SEAT Leon offers exhilarating performance as standard - in a car that is anything but. If you like your road served raw, brace yourself for a ride that'll leave you on the edge of your seat grinning for more.

The new SEAT Leon. From £11,295 on the road*

SEAT
auto emoción

seat.co.uk   0500 22 22 22

*Model shown is Leon 2.0 TFSI Sport with metallic paint at £16,320 RRP. Official fuel consumption for the Leon range in mpg (litres/100km): urban: 42.8 (6.6) - 23.2 (12.2); extra Urban: 62.8 (4.5) - 43.5 (6.5); combined: 54.3 (5.2) - 32.8 (8.6). CO2 emissions 141-206g/km.

EXPLORING THE TEXT

SEAT ADVERTISEMENT

1. What image of the car do you get, based on the photograph alone? What features of the photograph help to create this image?
2. Write down the advantages of this car that are suggested by the photograph and the text.
3. Study the text carefully. What words and phrases would appeal to men?
4. How much technical jargon is used? Why is it included in the text?
5. If you were the manufacturer of this car, would you be satisfied with this advertisement? Give reasons for your answer.

Use the following questions to analyse the Samsung advertisment on page 306.

EXPLORING THE TEXT

SAMSUNG ADVERTISEMENT

1. How does this advertisement capture your attention? Refer to the photograph and the different print sizes in your answer.
2. How many times does the manufacturers' name appear? Why?
3. Does it use a striking phrase? What is it and what does it suggest about the product?
4. What is the connection between the slogan and the photograph?
5. What claims does the advertisement make about the design, quality, and technology of the product?
6. How much factual information is included?
7. Is the price mentioned?
8. Who is the target audience?
9. What strikes you about the use of colour in this advertisement?
10. Write an assessment of this advertisement.

imagine compact but powerful

Like the stag beetle, the ultra slim, sliding Samsung E370 is deceptively powerful in comparison to its miniature proportions. With a 1.3 Megapixel camera, video recording, music player, Bluetooth, a 40MB internal memory and a large TFT LCD screen, it's hard to imagine it only weighs 85g. **samsungmobile.co.uk**

Samsung **E370**

Rest insured.

Your family, your home, your future. It's good to know that someone is always there, looking after the things that matter to you most. And at EBS, we do just that.

We offer a range of insurance services, from home and contents, life and critical illness to accident, illness and redundancy. You don't have to be an existing EBS customer and when you compare our rates against the others, you'll see that with EBS, you really are better off in the long term.

For more information on EBS Insurance Services call into your local EBS office today or call <<EBS*DIRECT*>> on 1850 654325, or visit our website at www.ebs.ie. And rest assured, with EBS Insurance, you're in safe hands.

You're better off in the long run.

EBS
BUILDING SOCIETY

www.ebs.ie
Chief Office: P.O. Box 76, 30/34 Westmoreland Street, Dublin 2.

Use the following questions to analyse the EBS advertisment on page 307.

EXPLORING THE TEXT

EBS ADVERTISEMENT

1 What service is advertised here? Can you get more information about it? How?

2 Why did the advertisers choose to use the image of a little girl holding a soft toy rather than a little boy holding a toy soldier?

3 How does the consumer respond to the image?

4 What is the link between the photograph and the service provided?

5 Are the colours used in the illustration warm or cold? What effect do they have on the reader?

6 Who is the target audience?

7 Give your opinion of the caption.

8 Comment on the impact of this advertisement.

Use the following questions to analyse the Iarnród Éireann advertisement on page 309.

EXPLORING THE TEXT

IARNRÓD ÉIREANN ADVERTISEMENT

1 What is the purpose of this advertisement?

2 What techniques are used to attract your attention?

3 Comment on the use of colour in the advertisement and the company logo.

4 How can you get more information?

5 Study the advertisement again. Do you think that it is a good way of promoting the service? Give reasons for your answer.

Daddy, what's a queue?

New ticket machines mean an end to queues.

Queuing for a ticket may soon be a thing of the past, thanks to the arrival of new automatic ticket machines.

And there are other improvements to look forward to. For example, First Class and CityGold tickets can now be booked on-line at www.irishrail.ie. We plan to extend this new service to more Intercity passengers in the coming months.

www.irishrail.ie

Iarnród Éireann

1 What product is advertised below?

2 Who is the manufacturer?

3 How does it capture your attention? Comment on the caption, the use of colour and the type of print used in your answer.

4 How much information is given in this advertisement?

5 Do you think that this is an effective advertisement? Explain your answer.

Use the following questions to analyse the Ski advertisement on page 311.

● ● ● EXPLORING THE TEXT ● ● ●

SKI ADVERTISEMENT

1 What is the most eye-catching part of this advertisement? Is it the name of the product, the photograph, the print or the use of colour?

2 What is the connection between the way the text is written and the product?

3 Who is the target audience? Explain your answer.

4 Why should you buy Ski yogurt, according to this advertisement?

5 Compare this with the advertisement for Tabasco sauce. Which of them do you prefer? Give reasons for your choice.

- Open a new section in your media folder, label it 'Advertisements' and begin your own collection of advertisements. Cut out an advertisement that you liked and explain why you thought it was effective.

- Find an advertisement aimed at teenagers. How are the teenagers depicted? Are they seen as popular, fun-loving and happy? Are they untidy, rebellious or problematic? Are they stereotyped? Why did the advertiser portray them in that way?

- Find an advertisement showing young women and place it in your media folder. How are young women portrayed in advertisements? Is it an accurate picture?

- Place an advertisement showing young men in your media folder. How are the young men depicted? Do you agree with the image?

- Do advertisements place pressure on young people? Explain your answer.

- Discuss your favourite advertisement with the person beside you. You may have seen it on television, on a poster, or in a magazine or newspaper. What made it memorable for you? Jot down your answers and then share them with the class. Make a list of the favourite advertisements and discover what made them popular.

- Design your own advertisements for:
  - a soft drink
  - a motor car
  - a mobile telephone
  - sports shoes
  - an expensive watch

You can draw or cut out pictures for your illustration.

PRESS ADVERTISING

Most newspapers contain advertisements. Many publications could not survive without the money generated from advertising. The advantages of press advertising are:

- They can be read by a wide audience
- They can be re-read later
- They can be quite detailed
- Illustrations can be used to attract attention
- Coupons can be included
- They can be placed at short notice

However:

- Newspapers and magazines are not kept for long
- The image on the page can be poor due to the low quality of the paper
- There may be other advertisements on the same page
- The use of colour in printed advertisements is expensive

CLASSIFIED ADVERTISEMENTS

Classified advertisements are the 'small' advertisements that are found in newspapers and magazines. They often appear under headings such as 'Situations Vacant', 'Pets', 'Lost and Found' and 'Articles Wanted'.

They use abbreviations, for example:

- ono. – or nearest offer
- fur. – furnished
- bdrms – bedrooms
- gdn. – garden
- s.a.e. – stamped addressed envelope

YOUR TURN

- Find the classified advertisement section in a newspaper and add it to your media folder.
- Imagine you have a bicycle for sale. It is four years old and has some scratch marks. Design your own 'small' advertisement based on the examples you have found.
- You have found a valuable ring while out walking. Send a notice to the lost and found section of the classifieds.
- Respond to the following advertisements:

BABY SITTER REQ'D, weekends only, 3 children. Experience necessary. Apply with refs to Box No. 4412

DOG WALKER REQ'D for two dogs, 7pm–9pm (Flexibility). No experience necessary. Box No. 3111

PART-TIME SHOP ASSISTANT REQ'D for busy sports shop. Experience not essential. Suit young person. Box No. 6688

ACKNOWLEDGMENTS

Bruce Wilmer for 'New Beginnings'; Morris Gleitzman for the extract from *Blabbermouth*; extract from 'The Shakespeare Stealer' by Gary Blackwood, published by The O'Brien Press Ltd, Dublin © Gary Blackwood; Wolfhound Press for 'His First Flight' by Liam O' Flaherty from *Short Stories of Liam O'Flaherty*; Constable & Co. Ltd for 'The Trout' by Seán Ó Faoláin from *The Finest Stories of* Seán Ó Faoláin; Kingfisher Books for 'The Greatest' by Michelle Magorian from *Ballet Stories*; Penguin Books for 'Charles' by Shirley Jackson; HarperCollins Publishers for 'All Summer in a Day' by Ray Bradbury; Vintage Books for 'First Confession' by Frank O'Connor from *Collected Stories*; Omnibus Books for 'Love Letters' by Kate Walker from *Changes and Other Stories*; Addison Wesley for 'The Scream' by Elizabeth Laird; Random House Publishers for an extract from 'Jurassic Park' by Michael Crichton; HarperCollins Publishers for an extract from 'The Lord Of The Rings' by J.R.R. Tolkien; Seddon Peak Pty Ltd for film review of *Babe*; Robin Klein for extract from *Hating Alison Ashley*; Pan Macmillan Australia Pty Ltd for extract from the *Great Gatenby* © John Marsden 1989 and the extract from *Misery Guts* by Morris Gleitzman © Morris Gleitzman 1991; A.P. Watts for 'Goodbye' by Carol-Anne Marsh, 'The Boy Without a Name' by Allan Ahlberg, 'The Loner' by Julie Holder, 'Fight' by Barrie Wade, 'Teacher' by Mary E. O'Donnell, 'What is…. The Sun' by Wes Magee, 'Winter' by L.A.G. Strong; Hilarity Art for the comic strip *Thin Ice*; 'Flashing Neon Light' and 'Sparrows' from James W. Hackett, from *The Zen Haiku and Other Zen Poems of J.W. Hackett*, Tokyo, Japan Publications; Judith Wright for 'Magpies' from *A Human Pattern: Selected Poems* (Ett Imprint, 1996); Omnibus Books Australia for 'Love Letters' by Kate Walker from *Changes and Other Stories*; Penguin Books for the extracts from *The Diary of Anne Frank*; Faber and Faber for 'Tich Miller' by Wendy Cope, 'The Trees' by Phillip Larkin, 'Blackberry Picking', 'Mother of the Groom', 'When All The Others' and 'Mid-Term Break' by Seamus Heaney, 'Back in the Playground Blues' by Adrian Mitchell, and 'Nice Work' by Judith Wright; Pan Macmillan Australia Pty Ltd for 'Thistles' by Ted Hughes, 'The Sea is a Hungry Dog' by James Reeves, extract from 'A Sequence of Poems for my Daughter' by Debi Hinton; David Higham Associates Ltd for 'Nettles' by Vernon Scannell and 'Miller's End' by Charles Causley; 'Empty Fears' by Brian Lee; 'Midnight Wood' by Raymond Wilson; 'Flannan Isle' by W.W. Gibson; Bloodaxe Books for 'I See You Dancing, Father' by Brendan Kennelly from *Familiar Strangers: New & Selected Poems 1960-2004* (Bloodaxe Books, 2004) www.bloodaxebooks.com; Brendan Kennelly for his translation of 'My Story'; 'The Pattern' by Paula Meehan, by kind permission of the author and The Gallery Press, Loughcrew, Oldcastle Co. Meath, from *The Man who was Marked by Winter* (1991); Allan Mackay for an extract from his short play *King Chicken*; Oxford University Press for extracts from *Across the Barricades* by Joan Lingard adapted by Ian Neville (Oxford Playscripts, 2003), copyright © David Neville 1990, reprinted by permission of Oxford University Press.

While every care has been taken to trace and acknowledge copyright, the publishers tender their apologies for any accidental infringement where copyright has proved untraceable. They would be pleased to come to a suitable arrangement with the rightful owner in each case.

For permission to reproduce photographs the author and publisher gratefully acknowledge the following: 304, 306 © Advertising Archive; 124, 153, 159, 247 © Alamy; 271 © Camera Press; 309 © Iarnród Éireann; 311 © Nestlé.

abstract nouns 119–20

Across the Barricades 258–68

acrostic poems 200

adjectives 177–83

adverbs 184–7

advertising 296–314

   adjectives in 178, 183, 300

Ahern, Cecelia 128–9

Ahlberg, Allan 204

All Summer in a Day 48–54

alliteration 191, 280

apostrophes 85–8

assonance 191

Babe (film) 168–9

'Back in the Playground Blues' 208

banner headlines 277, 278

Blabber Mouth 7–9

'Blackberry-Picking' 222–3

Blackwood, Gary 10–12

blank verse 191

book covers 108–10

book reviews 166–8

'Boy Without a Name' 204

Bradbury, Ray 48–54

broadsheets 274–8

capital letters 81–2

captions 277, 278

cartoons 291–4

   and pronouns 125

Causley, Charles 236

'A Cello' 201

characters in stories 91

Charles (short story) 45–7

classified advertisements 313

clichés 280

collective nouns 117–18

colour, in advertising 299

comedy 247, 250–3

comic strips 291–4

   and pronouns 125

commas 83–5

common nouns 114

conflict

   in drama 249

   in story writing 91–2

Cope, Wendy 202–3

covers of books 108–10

Crichton, Michael 92

Cross, Gillian 125

curriculum vitae (CV) 137

Demon Headmaster, The 125

descriptions 102–6

   adjectives and adverbs 177–87

diaries 163–5

Diary of Anne Frank 163–4

directions, writing 172–4

Doyle, Sir Arthur Conan 146–7

drafts 155–6

drama 19–22, 246–68

   comedies 247, 250–3

   modern drama 258–68

   production roles 268

   radio 23–5

   tragedies 247, 254–7

editor of newspaper 272

   letters to 287–9

editorials 285–6

'Empty Fears' 238

Espy, Willard R. 80

exclamations 81, 83

explanations, writing 172–4

expressive verbs 150

factual texts 5, 152–74

farce 247–8

Farjeon, Eleanor 191

features, in newspapers 277

'Fight' 210–11

fillers, in newspapers 277

film reviews 168–9

First Confession 56–64

first person 123, 124

'Flannan Isle' 241–4

'For Better or For Worse' 293

'Forest' 200

formal letters 134–9

Frank, Anne 163–4

free verse 193–4

full stops 81–2

future tense 148–9

Gibson, W.W. 241–4
Gleitzman, Morris 7–9
Going Home 19–21
Gold Cross of Killadoo 167
'Goodbye' 194
Greatest, The 38–43

haiku 196–7
Harry Potter and the Prisoner of Azkaban
   140–2
headlines 277, 278, 279–80
Heaney, Seamus 222–3, 229, 231, 232
Hinton, Debi 233
His First Flight 14–18
Hobbitt, The 180
Holden, Julie 206
Hughes, Ted 221

'I See You Dancing, Father' 226
'I Wandered Lonely as a Cloud' 218
imagery 192
instructions, writing 170–2
invitations, writing 128

Jackson, Shirley 45–7
journalism 273, 281–6
Julius Caesar 254–7
Jurassic Park 92–100

Kennelly, Brendan 216, 226
King Chicken 249–3

Laird, Elizabeth 70–5
Larkin, Philip 220
Lee, Brian 238
Lester, Richard 201
letter writing 127–43
   formal letters 134–9
   letters to newspapers 287–9
   personal letters 128–33, 141
limericks 121–2, 198–9
literary texts 4, 6–25
'Little Frog' 196
logos 298
'Loner, The' 206
Lord of the Rings 104–5
Lost World, The 146–7
Love Letters 66–9
lower case 298
lyrics 192

Magee, Wes 214
Magorian, Michelle 38–43
'Magpies' 195
Marsden, John 102, 186
Marsh, Carol-Anne 194
masthead 277, 278
Meehan, Paula 234
metaphors 192
'Midnight Wood' 240
'Mid-Term Break' 229
'Miller's End' 236
mime 248
Mitchell, Adrian 208
'Mother of the Groom' 231
'My Story' 216
mystery poems 235–44

names, as proper nouns 115–16
narratives 4, 28–9
narrators 28
nature poems 214–25
'Nettles' 228
'New Beginnings' 6
news agencies 273
newspapers 271–90
news-writing 281–6
nouns 113–22
novels 7–13, 90–110
   structure and features 91–2

O'Connor, Frank 56–64
O'Donnell, Mary E. 212
O'Faolain, Sean 33–5
O'Flaherty, Liam 14–17
onomatopoeia 192

past tense 148–9
'Pattern, The' 234
people, describing 102–3, 179–80
personification 192
places, describing 104–6
plays *see* drama
plot 91
poetry 189–244
   about family 225–35
   about mystery 235–44
   about nature 214–25
   about schooldays 202–13
'Poetry' (poem) 191
present tense 148–9

press advertising 313
press releases and conferences 274
proper nouns 115–16
pronouns 123–5
proverbs 120
punctuation 79–88
puns 280

question marks 81, 83
Quinn, John 167

radio drama 23–5
recipes, writing 170–1
Reeves, James 224
Reldas, Allison 200
report writing 157–62
reporting for newspapers 273, 281–5
review writing 166–70
rhythm 193
rhyme, in newspaper headlines 280
Rowling, J.K. 140–2

Scannell, Vernon 228
Scream, The 70–5
'Sea is a Hungry Dog' 224
seasons, describing 106–7, 216, 217
second person 123, 124
sentences 80–8
'Sequence of Poems for my Daughter' 233
setting of stories 91
Shakespeare, William 254
Shakespeare Stealer, The 10–12
shape poems 201
short stories 14–18, 27–77
    structure and features 29–30
similes 193
slogans 298
sonnets 195–6
speeches 55
'Spider' 200
stanza 193
statements 81, 83
Stevenson, Robert Louis 23–4
Strong, L.A.G. 217
sub-editors 272
sub-headings 277, 278
suspense in story writing 92
symbolism 193

tabloids 274–8
target audience 298
'Teacher' 212
tenses of verbs 148–9
texts 3–25
theme in story writing 92
third person 123, 124
'Thistles' 221
'Tich Miller' 202–3
Tolkein, J.R.R. 104–5, 180
tragedies 247, 254–7
Treasure Island 23–4
'Trees, The' 220
Trout, The 33–5
typography 279

upper case 298

verbs 145–60
verse, blank 191
verse, free 193–4

Wade, Barrie 210–11
Walker, Kate 66–9
weather, describing 106–7, 216
'What is ... the Sun?' 214
'When All the Others' 232
Where Rainbows End 128–9
'Wild Geese' 197
Wilmer, Bruce B. 6
Wilson, Raymond 240
'Winter' (poem) 217
Winter (story excerpt) 106
Wordsworth, William 218
Wright, Judith 195